MAUDSLEY MONOGRAPHS

HENRY MAUDSLEY, from whom the series of monographs takes its name, was the founder of the Maudsley Hospital and the most prominent English psychiatrist of his generation. The Maudsley Hospital was united with the Bethlem Royal Hospital in 1948, and its medical school, renamed the Institute of Psychiatry at the same time, became a constituent part of the British Postgraduate Medical Federation. It is entrusted by the University of London with the duty to advance psychiatry by teaching and research.

The monograph series reports work carried out in the Institute and in the associated Hospital. Some of the monographs are directly concerned with clinical problems; others, less obviously relevant, are in scientific fields that are cultivated for the furtherance of psychiatry.

Editors

1955–1962   Professor Sir Aubrey Lewis LLD DSC MD FRCP and Professor G W Harris MA MD SCD FRS
1962–1966   Professor Sir Aubrey Lewis LLD DSC MD FRCP
1966–1970   Professor Sir Denis Hill MB FRCP FRCPSYCH DPM and Professor J T Eayrs PHD DSC
1970–1979   Professor Sir Denis Hill MB FRCP FRCPSYCH DPM and Professor G S Brindley MD FRCP FRS
1979–1981   Professor G S Brindley MD FRCP FRS and Professor G F M Russell MD FRCP FRCP(ED) FRCPSYCH
1981–1983   Professor G F M Russell MD FRCP FRCP(ED) FRCPSYCH
1983–1989   Professor G F M Russell MD FRCP FRCP(ED) FRCPSYCH and Professor E Marley MA MD DSC FRCP FRCPSYCH DPM

Joint Editors, 1989 to present

Professor Gerald Russell   Professor Brian H. Anderton
MD, FRCP, FRCP (Ed.),   BSc., PhD
FRCPsych.

Assistant editors

Dr Glyn Lewis
BA, BSc., MB, MRCPsych.

Dr A. David
MPhil., MSc., MRCP, MRCPsych.

with the assistance of

Miss S. E. Hague, BSc. (Econ), MA

INSTITUTE OF PSYCHIATRY

Maudsley Monographs

Number Thirty-five

Arson
A Review of the Psychiatric Literature

By

ANN F. BARKER, BA, MB, BS, MRCPSYCH, MPHIL
Consultant Forensic Psychiatrist, Broadmoor Hospital

OXFORD UNIVERSITY PRESS
1994

Oxford University Press, Walton Street, Oxford OX2 6DP
Oxford   New York   Toronto
Delhi Bombay Calcutta Madras Karachi
Kuala Lumpur Singapore Hong Kong Tokyo
Nairobi Dar es Salaam Cape Town
Melbourne Auckland Madrid
and associated companies in
Berlin   Ibadan

Oxford is a trade mark of Oxford University Press

Published in the United States
by Oxford University Press Inc., New York

A catalogue record for this book is available from the British Library

Library of Congress Cataloging in Publication Data

Barker, Ann F.
Arson : a review of the psychiatric literature / by Ann F. Barker.
(Maudsley monographs ; no. 35)
Includes bibliographical references and index.
1. Arson—Psychological apsects. I. Title. II. Series.
[DNLM: 1. Firesetting Behavior—psychology. W1 MA997 no. 35 1994
/ WM 190 B255a 1994]
RC569.5.P9B3 1994 616.85'843—dc20 94-5631

ISBN 0 19 262526 8

Typeset by
Advance Typesetting Limited, Oxfordshire
Printed in Great Britain on acid-free paper
by Biddles Ltd, Guildford & King's Lynn

Acknowledgements

Only the salient findings from the non-clinical source of literature have been presented. I am grateful, however, to particular individuals for their help and guidance, including Mick Kemp of the Fire Department of the (then) DHSS, Ted Moxom from the National Association of Hospital Fire Officers, Professor John Gunn of the Institute of Psychiatry, and my personal assistant, Carole Andrews.

Tables

Figures

Contents

1 Introduction

This monograph aims to present a review of the psychiatric literature on arson and arsonists. It does not present original empirical research data.

The terms 'arson' and 'arsonist' have an emotive ring, like 'murder' and 'murderer', and indeed, until the advent of weapons of mass destruction in the twentieth century, arson was one of the most powerful methods of causing murder and mayhem. Fire itself has also been a universal symbol beloved of poets and artists from time immemorial. It is thus not surprising that psychiatric studies of arsonists are as old as psychiatric studies themselves: a fascination with 'abnormal' behaviour appears to be a 'normal' human phenomenon. Perhaps, at heart, this review most closely resembles a 'personal journey' through the literature on one form of criminal behaviour, towards an understanding of what that behaviour signifies.

In the quest for understanding of this behaviour, different images of arsonists have emerged at different periods. A pre-scientific description of an arsonist is that of the Old Testament hero, Samson, scourge of the Philistines, judge over Israel for 20 years, a somewhat reprehensible superman, reputed to have slain a lion with his bare hands and to have felled a thousand of his foes armed only with the jaw bone of an ass. Incensed one day that one of his lady-loves had been given away in marriage during his absence, Samson set upon revenge . . . 'So he went and caught three hundred jackals, and got some torches; he tied the jackals tail to tail and fastened a torch between each pair of tails. He then set the torches alight and set the jackals loose in the standing corn of the Philistines . . . And he burnt up standing corn and stooks as well, and vineyards, and olive groves . . . (Judges 15: 3). The grandiose scale of his revenge is characteristic of Samson; the grandiosity or 'hubris' of those dealing with fire is typified in the Greek myth of Prometheus, who stole fire from the gods, bringing it as a gift to mankind.

In nineteenth-century Europe, where arson was one of the *causes célèbres* for exemption from capital punishment, the view of the 'typical' arsonist could not be in more contrast: typically, she was viewed as a female domestic, barely into her teens, uprooted from her home and family, suffering with nostalgia. Fire was no more than a tool that was part of her daily working life. Later, following the influence of Freud, arsonists were seen as driven by a sexual motive. By the 1950s, Lewis & Yarnell (1951), in the most comprehensive of studies of arsonists, described the popular conception of the arsonist as a 'pale and yellow, insignificant creature', driven by 'an irresistible impulse'. Perhaps as courts took a rather more sceptical attitude towards the 'irresistible impulse', seeing crime in general as an 'impulse which has not been resisted' (Williams, 1953), the search for a wider selection of driving forces, or motives for arson became evident in the scientific literature. A recent perspective, in our cybernetic age with its doubts about the difficulty of communication, describes arson as a 'communicative' weapon (Geller, 1984).

Behind these studies, it seems to me, there is a search for an entity, an 'arsonist', who perpetrates the arson, and an attempt to isolate one single factor which drives the behaviour. Yet arson is no more than a behaviour, which, if medical terminology were used, could be called a symptom or a sign. It could, in psychiatric terms, be compared to an hallucination: hallucinations are known to occur in certain illnesses; probably, however, the majority of hallucinations are normal phenomena, hypnagogic hallucinations, experienced by 'normal' people.

The general purpose of the review is thus to consider the psychiatric literature and study the extent to which the arsonists portrayed differ in any significant manner from offender populations exhibiting other, different, disorders of behaviour, and whether from what is known, any facts emerge to typify 'the arsonist'. It aims to review the literature in the light of the statistics and research of other bodies which have practical interests vested in fire, such as the Fire Brigade, the Police, and the Insurance Agencies, focusing on areas of data, information, and knowledge about which there is agreement, and areas where there is considerable doubt.

In the light of these statistics, which reveal that very few of those who set fires are caught and that the majority of all fires are small, the review questions whether the term 'arsonist' deserves the mystique it has acquired, and also whether the term is not coloured by studies from such highly biased institutions as the Special Hospitals or Grendon Underwood Psychiatric Prison. Finally, it aims to delineate areas of future research which are of valid concern to the psychiatrist.

Whilst it proved relatively simple to obtain a comprehensive bibliography from a computer search of the medical literature, various facts became evident. First, certainly the largest survey of arsonists, that of Lewis & Yarnell in 1951, remains out of print, and is quite difficult to obtain.

Second, there are quite separate organizations with a pertinent interest in fire, such as the Fire Brigade, the National Insurance Agencies, and the Police and Home Office. In the UK these interested parties have been working quite separately with libraries such as that of the Fire Research Station at Boreham Wood, the Fire Prevention Association (headquarters of the National Insurance Agencies), and the London Fire Brigade (housing the library of British and foreign Fire Journals). Athough in the main their subjects of concern are technical detail rather than clinical interest, fire results from human malice, folly, ignorance, stupidity, and negligence, and a combined approach to the problems is welcomed in the new initiative of the Arson Prevention Bureau, set up in the UK in 1991. Other countries such as the USA have seen it prudent to tackle the problem of deliberate fire-setting by means of an 'Arson Squad' for some time. It is to be hoped that the new bureau will make the literature from diverse sources more easily available for future reference.

TERMINOLOGY

Synonyms for non-accidental fire-setters include fire-bugs, fire-raisers, incendiarists, arsonists, and pyromaniacs. Although all of them have a pejorative ring, today the actual choice of term tends to reflect the outlook of the user. Historically, the oldest is probably 'fire-brand', used as a noun to describe either the person or his weapon; a good example would be the 1611 Authorized Translation of the Bible, which leaves no doubt about the outlawed and unthinkable nature of the act: 'As a mad man who casteth fire-brands, arrows and death, so is the man who deceiveth his neighbour and saith ''Am I not in sport'' ' (Proverbs 26: 18). 'Arson' and 'incendiarism' are both comparatively new to the English language, incendiary being adopted a little before, and arson shortly after, the Great Fire of London in 1666; 'pyromaniac' was transported straight from the French to the English medical vocabulary in the early nineteenth century.

Arson today is a legal term, receiving its definition under the Criminal Damage Act, 1971. This Act covers damage to property in general, however it may have been caused. Section 1 of the Criminal Damage Act states under section 1(1) that it is an offence to damage or destroy property belonging to someone else without lawful excuse, although it is not an offence to destroy property if it is done in the honest or mistaken belief that the property is one's own; it is also an offence to act in a way that is reckless (which means, in law, knowing, or closing one's mind to, the obvious fact that there is a risk of damage) as to whether property would be destroyed or damaged. Section 1(2) covers damage to property which also endangers the life of somebody else: under this section of the Act, it is an offence, intentionally or recklessly, to destroy or damage property when at the same time there is either an intention or a recklessness about endangering the life of another person. Section 1(3) specifies that when the damage to property has been caused by fire, the offence shall be charged as arson. In practice, however, there is a tendency for cases of criminal damage to property by fire to be labelled simply as 'criminal damage', without arson being specified. The practical effect of this tendency is probably to minimize the number of cases of arson which appear in the Criminal Statistics.

It is also an offence under the Criminal Damage Act, 1971 to make threats that such damage would be carried out, in a manner such that the person threatened believes it likely that the threats would be carried out (section 2), or to have objects in one's possession with the intention of carrying out such damage (section 3). Simple criminal damage, whether or not caused by fire, is an offence that is triable 'either way', the limits being set by the cost of living: at present, for example, damage worth under £600 is triable only summarily in a magistrates' court. Similarly, threats to cause damage, or possessing objects with the intent to cause damage are triable either way, depending on the gravity of the circumstances. An offence that endangers life, under section 1(2), whether or not caused by fire, is triable only on indictment at the Crown Court.

Table 1.1. *Offences under the Criminal Damage Act, 1971*

Section 1	(1)	Intentional or reckless damage to property
	(2)	Damage endangering life
	(3)	Damage by fire termed arson
Section 2		Threats to damage property
Section 3		Possession of objects with the purpose of damaging property

In summary, intentional or reckless damage to property is an offence triable either way depending on the extent of the damage, and when it is caused by fire is termed arson. Intentional or reckless damage to property also intentionally or recklessly endangering the life of someone else—whether or not caused by fire—is triable only in the Crown Court, and, for arson, carries the maximum penalty of life imprisonment. Clearly the legal definition of arson covers the trivial to the most serious type of offence. Perhaps in recognition of this, it has become 'good sentencing practice' to call for a psychiatric report: Lord Justice Boreham in the Court of Appeal [*R*. v. *Calladine* (1975)] said: 'In cases of arson, it is the experience of this Court that it is wise to call for a psychiatric report so that one may judge the mental element in the perpetration of the offence. We regard it as certainly unwise to sentence without calling for such a report'. A further Court of Appeal judgement in 1980 from Lord Justice Stocker [*R*. v. *Hoof* (1980)] was that Courts should attempt to distinguish between intentional damage and reckless damage—a decision to be made by the jury—and that this distinction should be reflected in the sentence (Thomas, 1988). 'Intention' or 'recklessness' are thus clearly issues to which the psychiatrist should address himself in preparing a report for the Court; they are also, however, factors which should be addressed in assessing personality and mental illness, in patients who set fires, which have not been brought to the attention of the Courts, such as fires set in hospital.

Despite the attempts of the law to distinguish the most trivial from the most serious cases of arson, one fact should be noted in passing: the element of chance. It is Fire Brigade 'wisdom' that 'a large fire is one that started as a small fire and was not brought under control'. The final *quantum* of damage may thus bear little relevance to the initial intention, and a carelessly dropped match may wreak as much havoc as a fire deliberately started with gallons of petrol.

Turning from the modern legal definition to other terms for fire-setting behaviour, 'pyromania' was coined by Marc in 1833, a French physician of eminence whose views were quoted at the McNaughton trial (West & Walk, 1977); it described one of those 'instinctive and impulsive monomanias'—crimes against nature so monstrous and without reason, as to be explicable only through insanity, yet perpetrated by those apparently in full possession of their sanity—which have left us with the heritage of such terms as homicidal monomania, kleptomania, dipsomania, and so on. Within a few years, its existence was disputed. The German, Griesinger, whose works in translation were published in 1867, states forcefully: 'Away, then, with the term Pyromania, and let there be a careful investigation in every case into the individual psychological peculiarities which lie at the bottom and give rise to this impulse . . . To include (such cases) under the title of ''Pyromania'' is the necessary but evil result of a superficial classification . . .'

Pyromania, however, lives on, defined in the revised version of the third edition of the *Diagnostic and Statistical Manual of Mental Disorders of the American Psychiatric Association*: 'The essential features are deliberate and purposeful (rather than accidental) fire-setting on more than one occasion; tension or affective arousal prior to setting the fires; and intense pleasure, gratification or relief when setting the fires or witnessing or participating in their aftermath. In addition, there are fascination with, interest in, curiousity about, or attraction to fire and its situational context or associated characteristics (e.g., uses, consequences, exposure to fires). The fire-setting is not done for monetary gain, as an expression of socio-political ideology, to conceal criminal activity, to express anger or vengeance, to improve one's living circumstances, or in response to a delusion or hallucination.

Although the fire-setting results from a failure to resist an impulse, there may be considerable advance preparation for starting the fire, and the person may leave obvious clues. People with the disorder are often recognized as regular 'watchers' at fires in their neighbourhoods, frequently set off false alarms, and show interest in fire-fighting paraphernalia. Their fascination with fire leads some to seek employment or volunteer work in fire-fighting. They may be indifferent to the consequences of the fire for life or property, or they may get satisfaction from the resulting destruction'. Pyromaniacs are commonly known as fire-bugs.

Pyromania is thus narrowly defined, and the definition is not yet commonly used in Britain, where 'pyromaniac' and 'fire-bug' are alternatives more usually found in popular journalism. The medical literature tends to refer to 'arsonists' only in surveys of populations convicted by the Courts. Similar activities among patients are referred to as 'fire-setting behaviour', reflecting, perhaps, the ambivalence of doctors to charging their patients with criminal acts. Studies of children below the age of criminal intent, of course, use neutral terminology, of which again, 'fire-setting behaviour' is the most common. One recent euphemism to emerge from a Home Office report is 'vandalism by fire'. Outside the caring professions, however, the approach is blunter. The standard headline in Fire Brigade publications runs: 'It was arson!'

Intentional or reckless fire-setting is a matter of widespread interest, reflected in the number of different synonyms for the behaviour. One of the disadvantages for research, however, is that the presence of these various synonyms tends to obscure the fact that they are all manifestations of one and the same behaviour; that is, deliberate fire-setting.

Summary

Non-accidental fire-setters are termed: fire-bugs, fire-raisers, incendiarists, arsonists, or pyromaniacs. The crime of arson has a legal definition under the Criminal Damage Act, 1971, in which the psychiatrist should attempt to specify whether a clear 'intent', or 'recklessness' was the more likely motivation.

'Pyromania' has always been a controversial concept but likewise has a definition, in the *Diagnostic and Statistical Manual of the American Psychiatric Association*. A term recently coined is 'vandalism by fire'.

Any researcher should be aware that these terms refer to one and the same activity, that is, deliberate fire-setting. Since chance plays a very large part in the final size of the fire it is mistaken to portray those setting small fires as 'vandals' in contrast to 'arsonists', whose resultant fires have been large ones. In addition, one term rather than a plethora of terms for the same behaviour should be employed, in order to underline a basic fact of criminology, that an illegal activity is much more common than ever appears in the Criminal Statistics.

DEFINITIONS OF FIRE-SETTING BEHAVIOUR

'Normal' human interest in fire starts very young and is certainly a pre-school activity. Nurcombe (1964) found interest in fire to start between 2 and 3 years of age, and Block *et al.* (1976) considered it to assume increasing salience between 3 and 5. Kafry's (1980) study of normal schoolboys at the ages of 6, 8, and 10 found that fire interest was almost universal, supporting Lewis & Yarnell's (1951) observation that 'undoubtedly the incidence of children who play with fire is far greater than any statistics show'. Although remaining attracted by fire, none of the boys in Kafry's study continued to set fires after the age of 8, having achieved by that age a high level of understanding of its dangerous consequences.

Among children in particular, as Kosky & Silburn (1984) point out, there is therefore a need for a clearer definition of what is abnormal behaviour, since fire-lighting by children may range from simply occasionally playing with matches or fires to definitely malicious fire-setting. Their own definition was that the child had lit a fire causing damage to property or had persistently played with fire in a manner which parents were unable to control. Other studies among children have broader definitions: Stewart & Culver (1982) for example, excluded playing with matches, but included children who had set at least one fire, whether intentional or not; such definitions could easily embrace normal childhood behaviour since with fire, experiment may rapidly turn into disaster. More recent work in the USA, where there is a drive towards active intervention programmes for children who set fires, attempts to define characteristics of children which put them at risk for setting further fires, thus warranting intervention. Kolko & Kazdin (1989) found group differences between fire-setters and non-fire-setters, which included more curiosity about fire and involvement in fire-related activities in the past and present, being more frequently exposed to peers and family members who were involved with fire, and eliciting more adults' complaints or concerns about the child's fire behaviour.

Only one study—that of Geller & Bertsch (1985)—attempts a definition of abnormal fire interest and fire-setting behaviour for use among adults. Geller & Bertsch included setting a fire, threatening to set a fire, and setting fire to self or others, whether or not the patient had been charged with it. They also included sounding a false fire alarm or calling the Fire Brigade with a false report of fire, deliberately playing with matches or throwing lighted matches and cigarettes, but excluded careless smoking habits and also self-burning by placing lighted matches against the skin. Whether, in fact, the latter should be excluded, on analogy with the exclusion of self-mutilation from suicidal behaviour, is uncertain. Geller & Bertsch studied a psychiatric hospital in-patient group, where sounding fire alarms may often be viewed more as a desire to cause a commotion rather than a morbid interest in fire, but it has to be said that their precise relationship is unknown.

Bentley (1976), a Fire Officer, categorized false fire alarms into several groups, some of which would appear to have little overt connection with fire. Thus, apart from the mentally ill, false alarms are commonly set by children for excitement or after a long period of being alone indoors, for example. They are set by youths, 'rebelling against all authority, or wishing to impress others of similar immaturity'; by those affected by alcohol: 'Calls from them are frequently directed against the hostelry from which they have just tottered, or, not infrequently, been evicted'; by jokers, summoning the Fire Brigade to, for example, cinemas showing films such as 'The Towering Inferno' or to the Houses of Parliament on Bonfire Night. As a final group, Bentley included the purely 'malicious', the reasons for whose calls were diverse, but ranged from conducting a war of nerves against a neighbour, to emptying the Fire Station so that its safe was unattended, or to diverting the Fire Brigade so that a deliberate fire might get a good hold elsewhere. Firemen are not infrequently killed or injured by false calls to, for example, fast railway lines or main roads at night, and here the connection with the malice behind arson is evident. Little or no connection is obvious in the example of the little old lady who lived in a separate part of the house from her estranged family, who repeatedly gave calls of fire to her home just for the inevitable, if brief, company of the firemen, the only callers she ever had.

If there is confusion in the medical literature about the boundaries between normal and abnormal behaviour, it is in one sense no more than a mirror of the uncertainty in other fields, in Britain at least, about what constitutes 'nuisance' and what 'crime'. In 1980 a Home Office Working Party was set up to consider the problem of 'vandalism by fire'. Vandalism is not a criminal offence, as the Working Party pointed out; but with a commonly used definition of 'wilful damage to public and private property and amenities', vandalism by fire falls under the rubric of the Criminal Damage Act, as arson. Part of the difficulty encountered by the Working Party in gauging the extent of the problem stemmed from the different perspectives of the Fire Brigade and the Police. Fire Brigades define the cause of fires as of 'malicious or doubtful origin' and 'fires by children'; the Police interest lies in whether an offence has been committed, i.e., whether it is an arson fire. The Working Party noted that this hybrid entity— 'vandalism by fire'—'in its implications for fire incidence, casualties, and losses, currently constitutes the major counterweight to successes otherwise being achieved by conventional fire prevention activities to offset fire losses'.

Fire is expensive. The annual cost of the Fire Brigade services in 1989 was £894 million. Arson is expensive too, costing perhaps a third to a half of the total loss from fire: in 1990 the Association of British Insurers announced fire losses for Great Britain (excluding Northern Ireland) of £954 million (ABI, 1990). To the ratepayer at least, there can be little point in perpetuating the concept of 'vandalism by fire'. The American approach is much more pragmatic. Between the ages of 3 and 17 children are labelled 'juvenile arsonists or fire-raisers' and practical intervention programmes are set up to deter them. To anyone investigating the natural history or prognosis of an arsonist, lack of awareness of this entity 'vandalism by fire' is a hindrance. A consensus on a definition would be a helpful start in Britain.

Similarly, definitions of fire-setting behaviour are not merely of academic interest. Of nearly four hundred thousand emergency fire calls to the Fire Brigade in 1989, about one hundred thousand— approximately a quarter—were malicious false alarms (Report of the

Table 1.2. *Some Fire Brigade Statistics, 1989*

Total fire calls	383 000
Malicious false alarms	112 900
Convictions for false alarms	215

Chief Inspector of Fire Services, 1989). A grand total of 215 people that year were convicted for such offences. Clearly such false fire alarms not only cost public money and distract the emergency services from potentially disastrous fires, but they are also of consequence to the practising psychiatrist, for it is quite unknown whether they should be regarded merely as pranks, or as the portents of more serious offences, and the behaviour of potential arsonists.

Summary

Human interest in fire is normal in childhood; there is no clear definition of when fire-setting in childhood becomes abnormal. Among adults, only Geller & Bertsch's (1985) study attempts a definition of abnormal fire interest, which includes sounding false alarms, in itself a controversial concept. The lack of clarity on the subject is reflected by the general uncertainty about where vandalism by fire stops and arson begins. Again this is reflected in the fact that only in 1991 has an 'umbrella' organization, the Arson Prevention Bureau, been set up in Britain to pool the combined perspectives of the three bodies principally interested in fire: the Fire Brigade, the Police, and the Insurance Agencies, a parallel to the 'Arson Squads' already existing in the USA.

There are wide practical implications to this uncertainty about what is normal, a nuisance, or a crime, ranging from the national cost of fire, the cost of fire prevention, and prevention of pain and disfigurement, down to issues more commonly involving the psychiatrist such as predictions of future behaviour by the individual fire-setter (the issue of future dangerousness). Geller & Bertsch's definition would be a useful starting point for future studies.

THE PREVALENCE OF ARSON

A crime such as arson which consumes the evidence of its existence is always likely to be underestimated. It is also probably true to say that the prevalence of such a crime is only ever as high as the index of suspicion for it. The index of suspicion is currently running quite high, though certainly more so in the USA than in Britain, where, for example, an article in the *Observer Magazine* in 1974 ran the headline, 'Arson: the neglected crime'.

The need for a greater interest can be seen from the statistics of the National Fire Protection Association. In 1950 a total of 5600 fires were classified as 'incendiary or suspicious' in the USA, causing a monetary loss of $15 million. Lewis & Yarnell in their classic study of 1951, using the records of an affiliated association, the National Board of Fire Underwriters, could claim that arson was a rare crime, constituting no more than 0.1 per cent of serious offences. Twenty-five years later, however, in 1975, the figures of the National Fire Protection Association classified 144 100 fires as 'incendiary or suspicious' with a concomitant monetary loss of almost $634 million.

Arson has always existed, but there is little point in giving credence to early statements about its prevalence. The earliest textbooks on Fire Investigation for instance, date back only as far as 1945 (Barlay, 1972) and regular fire investigation was instituted only during the Second World War, when fear of sabotage made it a necessity.

Modern figures are only slightly less liable to give anything more than a random estimate of the prevalence of arson, fundamentally through lack of a systematized approach. To quote but two examples of this, all fires in the USA are considered 'innocent' until proved otherwise, in contrast to fires in Germany, where 'innocence' has to be proved. Arson rates in some jurisdictions are counted only after a court conviction has been recorded; in others, it is the suspicion of arson which is counted.

Reference has already been made to the entity of 'fire vandalism' in Britain, where all that may be said with certainty about prevalence is that the dark figure of crime for arson is very high. In 1989 the Police recorded among a total of three and three-quarter million notifiable offences nearly twenty-four thousand cases of suspected arson. Of these, 5643 were found guilty or cautioned (Criminal Statistics, 1989).

A breakdown of individual fires, however, shows that there were 96 033 fires in refuse and derelict vehicles; 11 000 fires in derelict buildings; some 1800 fires in schools, of which 60 per cent of the 67 'large' fires costing on average £220 000 each, were considered malicious; not to mention 1100 fires in letter-boxes—the latter being a highly unlikely site for spontaneous combustion.

It is necessary to emphasize these figures in order to stress that anything approximating an accurate estimate of incidence awaits, in

Table 1.3. *Notifiable offences recorded by the Police, 1989*

Total	3 870 700
Arson	23 715
Offences of arson cleared up	5643 (24%)
Fire Brigade Statistics, 1989	
Total fire calls	383 000

the first instance, a combined investigative approach by the prime interested parties, as is for example occurring in the USA, where Fire Brigades, Police, and Insurance Agencies are cooperating as 'Arson Squads'; a similar cooperative venture, the Arson Prevention Bureau, was set up in the UK in 1991.

Viewed from this perspective, the evidence from the medical literature can only be assessed as very misleading. As an example, prevalence rates among children are considered.

Helen Yarnell (1940) in the first study of fire-setting in children, quoted Wagner-Jauregg, who assumed the presence of a definite 'arson impulse' in all children, and did not offer a numerical value. Before undertaking her study, Yarnell had spoken with the Fire Chief for Manhattan, Bronx, and Staten Island, who reported that the 'Fire Department had many calls to put out small fires made by very young children, but that the fires were never serious and not frequently repeated, so that no significance was attached to them'. In Kafry's (1980) study of normal schoolboys aged 5–10, only 9 per cent of the fires caused by the children had been reported to the Fire Brigade. Turning to the medical literature, in the few studies where an incidence is given, problems of fire-setting are recorded as: Vandersall & Wiener (1970) 2.3 per cent; Kosky & Silburn (1984) 3.3 per cent; Jacobson (1985a) 2.45 per cent. Stewart & Culver (1982), apparently somewhat embarrassed at a prevalence of 14.3 per cent, felt that they had perhaps included children who had set fires of a relatively trivial nature—or alternatively that their clinic population was skewed to more severe cases and particularly to children with serious conduct disorders.

The main reason for the discrepancy emerged from a survey of public attitudes conducted by Winget & Whitman (1973), who found that fire-setting among children was not in general viewed as a medical problem; of 300 people randomly selected to be broadly representative of the population of Cincinnati, Ohio, who were asked

'What would you do if you had a child who repeatedly set fires?' only 20 per cent replied 'see a psychiatrist'. The second, and obverse, reason for the low estimates in the medical literature to date, is that inquiry about fire-setting behaviour has only very recently become a standard part of a routine medical 'history'. Geller & Bertsch's (1985) study was certainly thought-provoking: one-quarter of their hospital patients had at some time engaged in 'fire-setting behaviour' and 16 per cent had at some time actually set a fire. Albrecht (1990) in a personal series of 120 new judicial referrals for a psychiatric opinion, found that 35 per cent of all accused had a history of setting fire to themselves, others and/or property.

Should then, studies be undertaken to estimate more exactly the incidence of fire-setting among a normal population? Strachan (1981) raised the ethical objection that such an investigation 'might well suggest a pattern of dangerous behaviour to children who had not previously considered it'. Only one study in Britain has so far made the attempt. In a survey of Birmingham schoolboys aged 10−11, Wilson (Home Office Seminar on fires caused by vandalism, 1980) found that 19 per cent of boys had 'set a fire' within the previous 6 months (compared, for example, to 24 per cent who had broken a car radio aerial, or 56 per cent who had written on walls in the street). While limited funds are available, Strachan's objections would probably be upheld; resources would certainly be more profitably directed to intervention programmes, and the assessment of their effectiveness. There is, however, no reason why inquiry should not proceed more vigorously into the past history of general psychiatric patients, not only in order to obtain some estimate of incidence, but also to begin to acquire some idea of the natural history of fire-setting, albeit in a highly selected population. Such a survey by Kolko & Kazdin (1988) among 164 children attending a psychiatric out-patient clinic and 133 child in-patients, questioning the children's fire-setting behaviour over the previous 12 months, demonstrated the prevalence of fire-setting as 19.4 and 34.6 per cent respectively. Given an albeit fairly broad definition of fire-setting, the fire-setters were more likely to play with matches and show an interest in fire, and to have set more than one fire, although roughly half of the fires reported were committed by only one-fifth of the fire-setters.

Having stated that arson is a crime 'unusual, in that the event must first be carefully investigated, before one can ascertain whether the occurrence was indeed a crime' (Perr, 1979) and that the estimates in the medical literature can only be extremely inaccurate, no measure of the extent of arson is offered, except to quote Perr, who states 'anywhere between 10 and 75% of fires'.

In view of this, it is tempting to be dismissive and state that the widely reported and large increases in the number of malicious or arson fires are no more than a reflection of better and more determined investigation. It is also sensible not to extrapolate from the American crime figures or headlines, which run 'Arson, the growing problem', 'The arson epidemic', etc. Several lines of evidence do nevertheless, suggest that arson is increasing, and not just being increasingly detected. When rates of inflation have been taken into account, financial losses from fire have continued to rise, despite the fact that the number of fires caused by accident—from electrical failure and smoking for example—have remained static. Secondly, vandalism-arson—small, repetitive acts that slowly erode public amenities—had escalated to the extent that by 1978 the Home Office found it necessary to convene a working party to investigate the problem, which was then estimated to cost between £80 and £100 million per year. In Britain it would certainly be wrong to say, as does the USFA (1979) in its report to Congress: 'in many inner-city neighbourhoods, the gasoline splashed on an apartment door has replaced the gun as a way to settle quarrels'. It would be right to say, however, that there is at present a low awareness of the size of the problem. Seen in the context of a widespread phenomenon, the term 'arsonist' then perhaps carries a greater mystique than it rightfully deserves.

Summary

Arson is unusual as a crime, in that—consuming as it does the evidence of its existence—it requires a high 'index of suspicion' for the crime to be suspected before it can be established as such. Regular fire investigation is recent. Early figures for prevalence are therefore dubious. Modern figures in this country are also dubious and have been hampered by the separate investigative approaches of the Police, the Fire Brigade, and the Fire Insurance Agencies; consideration of the Fire and Criminal Statistics gives some indication of the disparity. Despite this uncertainty, arson is thought to be increasing.

Estimates of prevalence among children in the medical literature are likely to be highly misleading since fire-setting problems are not often referred to doctors and doctors do not often inquire about problems with fire-setting. There have been few surveys of normal populations, inquiring about prevalence and past fire-setting behaviour.

It would be a helpful start if psychiatrists were to ask their patients about fire-setting behaviour as a matter of routine.

CLASSIFICATION OF FIRE-SETTING BEHAVIOUR/ARSON

Vreeland & Waller (1979) state categorically that the lack of an adequate system of classification is a major contributory factor to our lack of understanding of fire-setting behaviour, pointing out that so far classifications have almost universally been based on the alleged motivation of the fire-setter and thus fail to incorporate many of the facts about arsonists which have come to light.

Very early classifications, such as that of Bucknill & Tuke (1879) led the way. They distinguished—1. Cases in which there was no marked disorder of the intellect (Emotional Insanity), subdividing them into (a) those in which there was no premeditation or design and (b) cases in which premeditation and design were present;—from 2. Cases with disorder of the intellect.

Modern classifications are based on the work of Lewis & Yarnell (1951) whose classic study of nearly 1200 fire-setters remains the most comprehensive work to date. Lewis & Yarnell did not consider arson for profit—the motive being fairly obvious—but concentrated on fire for 'mental reasons' and thus distinguished three main groups of fire-setters: the accidental, the occasional, and the habitual. Among these the motives might be:

(1) as a reaction against a social order which they believe is operating against their interests;
(2) to wreak vengeance against an employer;
(3) as a revenge for injured vanity;
(4) as a jealous rage reaction;
(5) as an opportunity to perform heroic endeavours as a fire-fighter;
(6) as a perverted sexual pleasure in the nature of a conversion of a sexual impulse into a special substitutive excitement.

Their Classification of Fire-setting because of mental reasons thus ran in outline as follows:

1. Accidental or Unintentional.
2. Delusional group.
3. Erotic group.
4. Revenge group.
5. Children's group.

Subsequent studies have mostly tended to modify and elaborate the original model of Lewis & Yarnell, the most recent of which is: *A Proposed Classification of Motives for Arson* (Prins *et al.*, 1985):

1. Arson committed for financial reward.
2. Arson committed to cover up another crime.
3. Arson committed for political purposes (e.g., for specific terrorist or similar activities).
4. Self-immolation as a political gesture.
5. Arson committed for mixed motives (e.g., in a state of minor depression (reactive), as a cry for help or under the influence of alcohol).
6. Arson due to the presence of an actual mental or associated disorder
   (a) severe depression
   (b) schizophrenia
   (c) 'organic' disorders (e.g., brain tumour, head injury, temporal lobe epilepsy, dementing processes, disturbed metabolic processes)
   (d) mental subnormality (retardation).
7. Arson due to motive of revenge:
   (a) against an individual/s (specific)
   (b) against society or others, more generally.
8. Arson committed as an attention seeking act (but excluding motives set out under (6) above).
9. Arson committed as a means of deriving sexual satisfaction or excitement.
10. Arson committed by young adults.
11. Arson committed by children.

A major hazard of a classification based on motivation is, as Durkheim (1897) pointed out, that 'human intention is too intimate a thing to be more than approximately interpreted by another person'. In a critical evaluation of their own proposed scheme on a series of 113 imprisoned arsonists, Prins *et al.* (1985) noted that while the majority of cases had been comprehensively documented, much of the information was speculative rather than factual, and there was often a naïve tendency to accept at face value the reasons advanced by the defendant. Thus in 13 per cent of their cases, three separate raters were unable to agree on the classification of the individual case; in some cases, no motive at all was apparent; furthermore, human motives are rarely pure, and in a number of cases it proved very difficult to discern a clearly defined single motive.

In addition, however, while most of the scheme is aimed at suggesting motive, as Prins *et al.* noted, some elements, e.g., (6) Arson due to the presence of an actual mental or associated disorder, rely purely on a description of mental states, which may merely affect motivation, rather than being in themselves motives. Virkkunen's (1974) study of the motivation for arson in schizophrenia had shown that where the underlying reason was at all discernible, it did not differ fundamentally from the basic causes which drive human behaviour in every day conflicts and desires. Some of the predicaments are most simply illustrated by a schizophrenic patient from Koson & Dvoskin's (1982) series, who, believing his grandmother to be a vampire bat, killed her; but then burned the house to destroy the evidence of the act. Arson in these circumstances should be labelled, to be more logical, arson in the presence of schizophrenia rather than arson due to the presence of schizophrenia.

Probably however, the ultimate embarrassment in any scheme such as Lewis & Yarnell's, which includes a subdivision 'Unintentional', is that found in the study of Harmon *et al.* (1985) where three of the women who had declared the fire was accidental were subsequently found guilty of arson by the Court. Nevertheless, many 'mental states', whether, at the extremes, dementia, or the play of childhood, will continue to be the 'motives' for arson, and the category 'Accidental' will remain among the list of motives for arson. Arson will remain criminal behaviour, and Courts will continue to request a reason for the defendant's actions. It is quite possible, Vreeland & Waller (1979) suggest, that ultimately, the motive for the arson will remain the most significant parameter in the act; yet, for the present, 'types' of fire-setters may be better identified by clusters of factors which occur together, presenting an image of arson as a multi-determined act, as described by Macht & Mack (1968). In practice, this is an approach with which few clinicians would tend to disagree.

Thus for the present, in the era of DSM IIIR, Vreeland & Waller propose that we should adopt an adequate descriptive system, before proceeding to a functional classification of fire-setters. Based on the philosphy of Social Learning theory, Vreeland & Waller suggest a description taking into acount four major aspects of behaviour:

1. Antecedent environmental conditions: referring to the individual's physical and social environment.
2. Organismic factors: describing personal variables such as age, sex, genetic factors, physical disabilities, associated behavioural and psychiatric problems, intellectual abilities, and cognitive style.
3. Actual fire-setting behaviour: which might include the degree and sophistication of preparation, the incendiary materials used, the location of the fire, the structures burned, and whether or not the fire-setter flees or remains at the scene of the fire.

4. The consequences of fire-setting: would include the actual or potential consequences of the fire-setting act which may serve to reward or otherwise maintain fire-setting behaviour. These would include the warmth and visual stimulation of the fire, the confusion which the fire creates, praise from peers for an act of defiance, praise from authority for helping to put out the fire, and economic gains.

The clear advantage of such a scheme, they suggest, is that it would provide a unified approach to classification, theory, and therapeutic change. Certainly any such multi-axial proposal must be preferable to increasingly lengthy lists of situations in which criminal behaviour can occur.

However, lest it be thought that medicine is alone in classifying arson by motive, the following categorization published by the US Fire Administration (1979) is reproduced for its broader perspective on the causes of arson. USFA 'identifies 24 different ''brands'', each with its own motivations':

1. Organized Crime:
   (a) Loan Sharking: High-risk clients are granted mortgages in the anticipation that they will not be able to make payments. When they seek a deferment, they are put in touch with a 'fire repair' company who leads them through a series of arson fires in lieu of mortgage payment.
   (b) Extortion: Arson is used for extortion, business takeover, and terror.
   (c) Cover Crime: Arson is used to cover-up a secondary crime.
   (d) Strippers: Strippers go into a newly or partially renovated building and pour accelerants down pipe chases, which they ignite. To extinguish the fire, fire fighters have to expose the plumbing, wiring, etc. Following extinguishment, the strippers return and remove wiring, plumbing, and fixtures.

2. Insurance/Housing Fraud:
   (a) Over-insurance: Property values are artifically inflated by trading a building among a ring of associates, with little actual cash changing hands as the value of the building increases on paper. Insurance is written for each 'paper' stage.
   (b) Parcel Clearance: Arson is used to destroy a building to create land for a new building or to expand an existing building adjacent to the parcel.
   (c) Gentrification: Low income tenants are 'evicted' through a series of small fires permitting the landlord to collect

insurance money to rehabilitate the property for high income ('gentry') tenants paying increased rent.

(d) Blockbusting: Arson is used to remove stable tenants to permit speculators to purchase housing at low cost and to justify rehabilitation support monies.

(e) Tax Shelters: Buildings are purchased in order to sell the tax depreciation allowance to persons seeking tax shelters. After the building is depreciated, it is burned for insurance money.

(f) Stop Loss: Speculators purchase property in anticipation of rapidly inflating housing markets. When the market does not develop the owner turns to arson to earn a profit.

(g) Anti-preservation: Buildings which cannot be torn down due to historic preservation restrictions are torched to provide the justification for demolition.

3. Commercial:

(a) Stop Loss: Restaurants, retailers, car dealers, and super-markets use arson to stop business losses and pay off indebtedness.

(b) Inventory Depletion: The small stable business can be purchased by persons of criminal intent. The good will of the business is used to over-order supplies and goods which are then removed from the store. Utility bills and taxes are allowed to go unpaid. The arson fire is used to cover-up the absence of the original inventory.

(c) Modernization: Business men with outmoded machinery modernize their plants with the proceeds from an arson fire.

4. Residential:

(a) Relocation: Homeowners who have difficulty finding buyers turn to arson. This practice is particularly prevalent among mobile home owners in remote construction sites.

(b) Redecorating: Smoky grease fires causing little structural damage but depositing grease and soot in the kitchen are used to collect insurance monies to finance redecoration.

(c) Public Housing: Arson puts the 'victim' at the head of the waiting list for an apartment and results in a furniture allocation.

(d) Automobile: Automobile arson is used to pay off indebtedness to finance the new car, or to cover a theft.

5. Psychological:

(a) Children: Children are motivated by curiosity or by emotional problems to play with matches and set fires.

    (b) Juveniles: Juveniles are motivated by curiosity, peer pressure, or challenges of other adolescents to set fires.

    (c) Revenge: Adults motivated by revenge, spite, or jealousy 'get' their opponent by burning a dwelling or personal property.

    (d) Pyromania: Persons suffering severe emotional problems set fire under delusionary influences.

    (e) Political: Extremist groups use arson as a method of intimidation and expression of anger, or to collect insurance to finance their political activities.

Following the precepts of Vreeland & Waller, an attempt will be made in the following pages to define the characteristics of arson as they appear from literature, under the following headings:

1. Characteristics of arsonists.
2. Characteristics of the fire.
3. Motives for arson.

Summary

Classifications are almost all based on the motive for the fire, the most modern, that of Prins *et al.* (1985), being little more than an elongated list, an elaboration of the 'classic' model of Lewis & Yarnell (1951). The disadvantages of a system that classifies by motive are that human intentions are difficult to gauge with certainty, and that motives are usually mixed and multiple. In addition, present classifications include categories which are descriptions of 'mental state' under the rubric of 'motivation'. The longest 'list' or 'classification', that of an American Arson Squad, is presented as an example of the extreme to which this form of classification may be taken.

    An alternative method of classification, as proposed by Vreeland & Waller (1979), is based on a multi-layered descriptive system.

    Future classifications are likely to retain the motive for arson as the linchpin for the classification, but need to be elaborated in terms of a multi-axial system of description, analogous to that found in DSM IIIR. Such a system emphasizes the notion of the arson as merely a 'symptom', to be viewed in the context of the whole person, not only to delineate different 'syndromes' of arsonists, but also to identify individual points of therapeutic intervention and future dangerousness.

2 Characteristics of arsonists

AGE

Arson has long been considered a crime of youth. To quote Bucknill & Tuke (1879): 'In short, as Marc concludes, incendiary acts are chiefly manifested in young persons, in consequence of the abnormal development of the sexual functions, corresponding with the period of life between twelve and twenty'. While not so certain of the cause, modern figures from the USA and Britain also emphasize the youth of the subject, and are impressively similar.

In Britain, in 1978, of those found guilty of, or cautioned for arson, 33 per cent were under 13 years, 28 per cent aged between 14 and 16, and 17 per cent between the ages of 17 and 20 (Home Office, 1980). Thus, of all those found guilty of, or cautioned for arson that year, 77 per cent were aged under 21. It has to be said, of course, that in terms of criminal success, youth carries the liability of inexperience, and thus the likelihood of being caught. Nevertheless, it would be flying in the face of experience in all other fields of crime to suggest that only youthful arsonists are apprehended, and that the figures are therefore very biased.

The majority of those serving prison sentences for arson are also young. In Britain in 1984 (Criminal Statistics) of the total of 528 males, 254 were aged under 21, and 274 were aged over 21. The percentages for the different age groups are shown in Fig. 2.1.

In summary, the percentage of those imprisoned for arson is fairly similar to those arrested for arson: 77 per cent of those arrested are under 21 and 65 per cent of those imprisoned are under 25. Women arsonists represent only 7 per cent of the prison population of arsonists, with numbers too small to invite any observation.

Based on arrest figures, Lewis & Yarnell (1951) in a survey so impressively large that it invites credence, felt able to state that the greatest incidence of fire-setting lay between the ages of 16 and 18. Without specifying a precise age, evidence for arson as a predominantly juvenile crime may also be derived from practical intervention programmes with juveniles in the USA. McKinney (1983), reporting on a community project in Texas for children

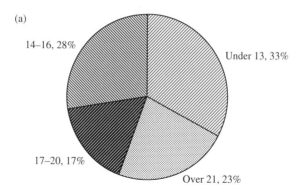

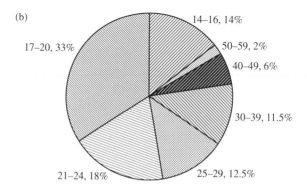

Fig. 2.1. Breakdown by age of males cautioned, arrested, and imprisoned for arson.
(a) Per cent arrested or cautioned, by age; (b) per cent imprisoned, by age.

between the ages of 3 and 17, noted the financial savings which had occurred. Although not wishing to attribute all of the success to the intervention programme, he observed that financial losses in Houston had fallen by 32 per cent (equivalent to £6 million) while over the same period, financial losses from fire had increased by 18 per cent in the surrounding countryside.

Turning to the medical literature, it is immediately apparent that among adults referred for a psychiatric opinion, the average age of arsonists is statistically above 'the norm' for the offence; in studies which have controls, arsonists are not invariably younger.

Thus the mean ages quoted are: Hurley & Monohan (1969), 25 years 10 months; Soothill & Pope (1973), 29 years, range 15−73; Virkkunen (1974), the majority were aged 21−30; 24.4 years; Bradford (1982), 30.3 years; Hill *et al.* (1982), 26 years; Koson &

Dvoskin (1982), 28.5 years; Yesavage *et al.* (1983), 24 for the mentally ill and 28 years for the not-mentally-ill group; 28.9 years; Molnar *et al.* (1984), solo arsonists 28.6 years, but 34 per cent of those with partners were aged 16—20. O'Sullivan & Kelleher (1987): prisoners (mean age 23 years 9 months) were significantly younger than patients (mean 31 years 5 months). The mean ages of female arsonists studied are: Tennent *et al.* (1971), Broadmoor, 28.9 years; Moss Side, 21.3 years, Rampton, 25.7 years; and Harmon *et al.* (1985), 34.7 years. Bradford also noted that the females in his series were more evenly distributed across the age spectrum whereas the males peaked in early adulthood or late adolescence. Geller & Bertsch's (1985) study of psychiatric in-patients gave a mean age of 30 years, but an age range of 12—63 years.

Amongst children referred to psychiatric clinics, the predominant age for fire-setting appears to be in later childhood, although the evidence from the literature is not entirely clear: Yarnell (1940): 60 per cent aged between 6—8, 35 per cent between 11—15. Vandersall & Wiener (1970): range 4—18. Strachan (1981): 21 per cent aged 8—11, 59 per cent aged 11—14, 19 per cent aged 14—16. Stewart & Culver (1982): 74 per cent under 10, 26 per cent over 10. Kuhnley *et al.* (1982): mean age 11 years, SD 2.12. Bumpass *et al.* (1983): range 5—14 years. Heath *et al.* (1983): under 12, 78 per cent, 13 or over 22 per cent. Kosky & Silburn (1984): range 5—16, mean 10.5 years. Kolko & Kazdin (1985): range 6—13, mean 9.9 years. Jacobson (1985a): bimodal age distribution at 8 and 13 years.

What may be inferred from this? Firstly, the majority of arsonists who are caught and sentenced appear to fall in the hiatus between adolescence and adulthood and also seem rarely to be referred for a medical opinion. Secondly, there can be no common denominator to an offence which can occur between the ages of 4 and 73. Thirdly, there is very little information about the 'natural history' of arson: in adult studies which report previous convictions for arson, it is unclear at what age they took place.

Superficially at least, it would appear, as it did in the nineteenth century, that arson resembles most other crimes and is mainly a feature of adolescence, but is 'available' at any age, and amongst females the diversity of ages is particularly apparent. However, the matter awaits clarification.

Summary

Fire-setting behaviour is recorded to occur between the ages of 4 and 73; a common denominator to an offence with such an age range is unlikely. Those detected committing arson are young; 33 per cent of all those arrested or cautioned for arson are under 13; 77 per cent of those cautioned or arrested are under 21, and 65 per cent of those imprisoned are under 25. Practical intervention programmes with juvenile arsonists in the USA have led to considerable financial savings. However, arsonists would not appear to differ significantly in this respect from any other type of offender, since overall the peak age for crime is 15 years.

The majority of those committing the offence are not seen by doctors; adults reported in the medical literature are older than the 'norm'. Although a commonsense interpretation of the Fire Statistics suggests that fire-setting is relatively common in youth, there is little scientific evidence to support this, and thus little precise knowledge about the natural history of the offence, other than the general observation that the vast majority of offenders grow up and abandon their delinquent behaviour; there is at present no evidence to suggest that arsonists differ from other types of offenders in this respect.

RATIO OF MALES TO FEMALES

Although a cursory glance at the literature suggests that fire-setting has shifted from being the predilection of young female domestics in nineteenth-century continental households to a highly masculine preoccupation in the mid-twentieth century, the highest estimate of female offenders is 37 per cent (Mönkemöller, Germany, 1912) with slightly lower estimates giving incidences of 35 per cent (Schmid, Switzerland, 1914) and 34 per cent (Marc, Paris, 1833), all quoted in Lewis & Yarnell.

Baker (1892), observing the comparative rarity of female arsonists in Britain in comparison with Europe, commented that in Britain women were 'rarely suspected and . . . treated with leniency if arrested'. Arson in Britain at that period still potentially attracted the death penalty, whereas in Europe pyromania had been equated with insanity and had thus become one of the *causes célèbres* for exemption from capital punishment. Throughout the nineteenth century in Europe, therefore, it would have been safer to charge women with arson, from the point of view of their ultimate punishment.

The typical female arsonist of nineteenth-century Europe appears to have been a young girl barely into her teens, uprooted from her family into a domestic position far from home. Viewed in context, however, in the mid-nineteenth century, following the role of agricultural labourer, the position of domestic labourer was the second most common occupation, and of domestics, half were women. 'Nostalgia' is cited as a common motive for arson in the nineteenth century, and it is quite possible that incidents for such a reason were higher in Europe, which had only recently seen the French Revolution, than in Britain with its much more tolerant acceptance of the social *status quo*. Lewis & Yarnell, conducting their survey in 1951, and in a different continent, considered that the steadily rising social status of the domestic had removed the need for rebellion from a formerly under-privileged group. Thus it is quite possible that fire-setting, which was certainly very much a natural tool for young European domestics, being part of their daily occupation and a mode of attack needing very little physical strength, has changed its incidence among men and women as a result of changing social circumstances.

An underestimation of females in the statistics is demonstrated by Tennent *et al.* (1971) whose survey of female arsonists in Special Hospitals revealed that only 46 per cent of them had ever been prosecuted for their offences. Given that the few surveys of female arsonists do tend to reveal a higher proportion with a more severe psychopathology, which would tend to lead them away from prosecu-tion in the criminal justice system, recent figures probably continue to underestimate the number of women who set fires. A recent survey by Harmon *et al.* (1984) solely of female arsonists may indicate that, in an era of 'sex equality' women are not only increasingly criminally active, but also increasingly prosecuted for their crimes.

The number of females reported in studies from child psychiatric cohorts tend to be very low; those from the adult cohorts are more variable, and it has already been noted that among adult females there is no especial age range for the crime of arson. Geller & Bertsch's (1985) study of a history of fire-setting among adult psychiatric in-patients was remarkable, however, in producing an equal number of males and females with a past history of such behaviour, and their findings await replication before any conclusions can be drawn.

Lewis & Yarnell (1951): 14.8 per cent were female. Soothill & Pope (1973): 4 per cent of females charged with arson. Virkkunen (1974): 10 per cent were female. Bradford (1982): males 76 per cent and females 24 per cent (Bradford quotes a high proportion of Indians in that area, with an apparently different sex distribution for crime). Yesavage *et al.* (1983): 4 per cent female. Molnar *et al.* (1984): 3 per cent of partner arsonists and 18 per cent of solo arsonists were female. O'Sullivan & Kelleher (1987): 23 per cent of fire-setters from the hospital series were female.

Girls in the series reported by child psychiatrists: Yarnell (1940): 3 per cent. Vandersall & Wiener (1970): 5 per cent. Strachan (1981):

1 per cent. Gruber *et al.* (1981): 10 per cent. Stewart & Culver (1982): 6 per cent. Kuhnley *et al.* (1982): 7 per cent. Bumpass *et al.* (1983): 7 per cent. Kosky & Silburn (1984): 3 per cent. Kolko & Kazdin (1985): 28 per cent. Jacobson (1985a): 16 per cent.

In one area of fire interest, however, males appear likely to continue to predominate. There are still only forty-five women among six and a half thousand operational fire-fighters in the London Fire Brigade.

Summary

Most of the illegal behaviour that is prosecuted is carried out by males. Despite the prominence accorded female arsonists at some historical periods, two-thirds of arsonists are always recorded as having been male. Female arsonists may have been given more prominence in the European literature in the past as pyromania was one of the *causes célèbres* for exemption from capital punishment; alternatively, female arsonists may have been prosecuted for arson less frequently than males in Britain and America, producing a lower incidence. Cultural factors such as the employment of female domestics, to whom fire was, in the past, a 'natural tool' may have affected the ratio of males to females. Contemporary trends, such as 'the equality of the sexes' may again vary the ratio by tempting women to commit crimes, encouraging alcoholism and thus crime among women, and favouring the prosecution of women for criminal offences.

Females are infrequent in modern child psychiatric cohorts. The only adult in-patient psychiatric study, however, shows an equal sex incidence. The ratio of male to female fire-setters is thus uncertain. A replication of Geller & Bertsch's (1985) in-patient survey would be useful.

PARENTAL BACKGROUND

Many, and wise, words have been written on the parental homes in which juvenile delinquents have been raised. In this respect, child and adolescent fire-setters are no different from other delinquents, though it is perhaps worth stating the obvious. From the medical literature it is almost a *sine qua non* of childhood fire-setting that the parental background of the child is heavily marked by pathology, and in the rare cases where it is absent, some other potent misfortune should be sought as laying the seed for this particular delinquent behaviour. The figures for 'pathological parenting' are as follows.

Among children referred for psychiatric assessment

A. Without control groups

Helen Yarnell's (1940) study of the younger fire-setters (aged 6–8) states 'In every case the child had been deprived of love and security in his home life. Some were children from boarding homes, who had not succeeded in finding any one person whom they loved and with whom they could identify. In the children coming from their own homes, there has always been some serious traumatic factor, such as an unsympathetic step-parent, with favouritism shown to step-siblings, an invalid and selfish parent, the absence of a father, or presence of 'boy-friends' of the mother. Some children had been placed temporarily in institutions, which to them represents, often correctly, rejection by their parents, which the child can never forgive'. Kanner (1957) noted that 'the combination of unhappiness over maternal perfectionism or outright rejection and disappointment in the father, augmented sometimes by sibling rivalry, recurs in our cases with surprising regularity'. In Lauretta Bender's (1959) series of children and adolescents who have killed, the six children who caused death by fire came 'from very disturbing home situations'. Vandersall & Wiener (1970) noted that, for their 20 children 'a mature, effective and consistently available father was not present in the home of any of these children', and mothers were 'to varying degrees affectively distant, rejecting, ineffective, and in some cases over-protective'. Fine & Louie (1979) recorded that seven out of 11 juveniles came from broken homes, and six had parents with severe psychopathology including suicide, homicide, psychoses, and alcoholism. Gruber *et al.* (1981) reporting on 90 children in residential treatment, noted not unnaturally, a family constellation of 'substantial social chaos and instability'. Similarly Strachan's (1981) cohort from a Scottish juvenile court showed as a 'marked feature' the high prevalence of unemployed or absent fathers; only 44 per cent of children were living with both their own parents. Two-thirds of Stewart & Culver's (1982) children had experienced disruption of their family life by parental fights, divorce, or desertion, and 24 per cent had been abused by one or other parent.

B. With control groups

Heath *et al.* (1983) found broken homes numerous (56 per cent) both in fire-setters and non-fire-setters; Kosky & Silburn's (1984) series had two-thirds of fire-setters coming from homes with parents who had separated, compared with one-third in non-fire-setters; Jacobson's (1985a) study noted abnormal family life affecting 91 per cent of fire-setters, with parental discord and inadequate or inconsistent supervision twice as frequently as for non-fire-setters.

Parents of normal children who play with fire

Kafry's (1980) study of normal schoolboys who played with matches noted that the mothers of children who had given up fire play reported better intra-family and inter-friend relationships than those of the children who were still playing with matches; in particular, fathers of the match-play group reported their sons as more mischievous and negative on many more behaviours than the mothers did. In terms of 'limit setting' parents of the match-play group used both more harsh punitive methods such as shaking the boy and some also reported severe physical punishments, or alternatively ignored the problem as a punitive method.

As a preliminary finding among these 45 per cent of normal children still playing with matches after starting school, Kafry noted the same parental tendencies: 'match-players came from more deprived families relative to those who did not, a relative deprivation reflected by parents' marital status, education, occupation, and residential area as well as in terms of family interpersonal relationships'.

One aspect of fire symbolism commonly used in interpreting fire-setting has been the God-like power of fire, whether in the quest for an absent father or in rebellion against a 'rejecting authority figure' such as school or hospital. In terms of the practical management of fire-setters, some useful strategies devolve around an attempt to provide a temporary father substitute. Among child fire-setters, for example, the 'Minneapolis experiment'—a community project for juveniles—involves providing a volunteer 'big-brother' for at least a year (Baizerman & Emshoff, 1984). In the treatment of manic fire-setters in hospital, Gunderson (1974) advocated a clear paternalistic approach, setting firm limits for the patient. Similarly, Lewis & Yarnell indicated that fire-setting would continue until the intervention of an 'external authority' occurred, to bring it to an end. Whether or not fire-setting can be correctly, psychodynamically, interpreted as an unconscious quest for the missing parental control, it is certainly in any event too dangerous an activity to permit anything but an authoritarian approach. Webb *et al.* (1990) describe a collaborative pilot programme for juvenile fire-setters in New York City involving the fire department and the mental health services; initial screening for future risk of fire-setting by the child is carried out by the fire marshall, and in instances of little risk, the case is managed by a fire-safety educational programme. Where the child is considered to be at greater risk of future fire-setting, the family is not only referred to a mental health clinic, but also followed up by the fire department, should the family fail to engage in treatment or drop out of treatment too early.

Amongst adult fire-setters reported in the literature, the same pattern of parental pathology is present, although, as with child fire-setters, it is unclear whether fire-setters are more severely deprived than controls in this respect.

Hurley & Monohan (1969): only 20 per cent had complete parental homes without recorded pathology, but this was not statistically different from controls. Tennent *et al.* (1971): there was significantly more separation from the parents before the age of 3 in arsonists than controls ($p > 0.05$). Foust (1979): in a series of 12 arsonists, the family history was replete with alcoholic, absent or even abandoning parents, physical and verbal cruelty, and condonation of fire-setting behaviour. Bradford (1982): 67 per cent were reared by their natural parents, and reported parental abuse less frequently than controls. Yesavage *et al.* (1983): of mentally ill arsonists, 63 per cent of fathers and 37 per cent of mothers were absent during childhood. Molnar *et al.* (1984): in the family data, partners differed significantly from solo arsonists only through the fathers' more consistent presence in the home in the former. Harmon *et al.* (1985): only 30 per cent were raised in a two-parent family.

Summary

The childhood background of fire-setters seen by psychiatrists is noted for its deprivation, both in child and adult clinics. The only study of the parental background of 'normal' children with pronounced match-play is similarly noted to be more deprived than that of the children who have abandoned the behaviour. Whether or not the interpretation of fire-setting as an unconscious quest for a missing authority figure is correct, the suggested management of fire-setting, because of its dangerousness, is along 'paternalistic' or authoritarian lines such as firm limit setting.

The pattern of 'parental deprivation' is a normal phenomenon in offending behaviour, and arsonists do not appear to differ significantly from other offenders in this respect. The majority of arsonists are undetected, however.

WORK HISTORY

'We find no instance of a man resorting to fire-setting while doing work in which he was interested and felt satisfied' (Lewis & Yarnell, 1951). Two aspects of the work history are most commonly sought by fire investigators suspecting arson among employees in the work place: 'grudge' and boredom. Envy, resentment, or ill-will are frequent motives for arson amongst those who have recently been dismissed from work or who simply bear a grudge against another employee. Classically, the most common target was the farmer's haystack, ignited by the farm labourer who had been sacked the previous day. Monotony or lack of recognition are similarly common motives among those with tedious occupations, such as orderlies in hospitals, night clerks, caretakers, and night watchmen. Elaborating on this theme of recognition, the desire to be seen as a hero, Cooke & Ide (1985) advise fire investigators to be aware that employees may themselves report a fire which they have started, either because they were seeking praise or reward, or 'because they started a fire, intending it to remain small, and then panicked when it became apparent that the fire was developing more rapidly than expected'.

Boredom, however, repeats itself commonly as a motive among vandals and the unemployed, who with some anomic disaffection appear, as Prins *et al.* (1985) noted, to be motivated by looking for 'kicks, and an element of getting back at a society that did not seem to care about them'. Certainly, when the work history of those referred for a psychiatric opinion is considered, its poverty is remarkable. Commenting on this in 1951, Lewis & Yarnell could state that 'in the protected environment of an institution we find that especially the pyromaniac group', (who by their definition constituted 60 per cent of the sample) 'develop into the most reliable and efficient workers. Others, once they had found suitable work which satisfied them and offered them protection and security, were able to settle down and apparently were in no further trouble with the law'.

Hurley & Monohan (1969): showed no difference between arsonists and a group of Grendon controls, only 22 per cent of whom held jobs regularly for longer than 1 year. Seventy per cent had deteriorating work records at the time of the offence. Inciardi (1970) among a cohort of paroled prisoners in New York State, found that 88 per cent were unskilled labourers, 21 per cent skilled and semi-skilled labourers, 5 per cent professional business or white collar workers, and 5 per cent had no occupation. Hill *et al.* (1982): at the time of the offence, only 37 per cent were employed, and 67 per cent of the series were characterized as unskilled labourers; this was not, however, significantly different from a control group of assaultive offenders. Bradford (1982): 58 per cent of the arson group were unskilled workers compared with 28 per cent of controls; no clerical, technical, administrative personnel, or small business proprietors were found in the arson group compared with 28 per cent of controls. Fifty-nine per cent compared with 56 per cent of controls were unemployed at the time of the offence—not a significant difference. Yesavage *et al.* (1983) comparison of mentally-ill and not-mentally-ill arsonists in the area of Bordeaux gave an overall unemployment rate of 38 per cent, whilst 32 per cent of the total were labourers. In the Molnar *et al.* (1984) study comparing 'partner' and 'solo' arsonists, fully two-thirds of those arrested on their own were supported by welfare or disability payments, in contrast to only 27 per cent of those arrested with a partner. O'Sullivan & Kelleher (1987) found no difference between prison and hospital samples, 78 per cent of both groups being unemployed. Harmon *et al.* (1985) study of female arsonists showed that only 11 per cent were employed at the time of the offence, and that these three women were in fact the only ones to have completed a course of higher education; 22 per cent of the series had never worked, correlating with those who had had the least education. Tennent *et al.* (1971) study of female arsonists in Special Hospitals however, showed no difference between arsonists and controls in terms of their work records.

Clearly no profession is exempt. Fire Officers refer to themselves in jest as 'sublimated pyromaniacs' (personal communication): Lewis & Yarnell had a series of 90 volunteer firemen who deliberately set fires. Le Couteur's findings (Fry and Le Couteur, 1966) from Broadmoor Hospital included a policeman, 'who by hysterical dissociation had set fires and committed crimes and then, being first on the scene, would set about solving these crimes with great rapidity'.

Vreeland & Levin (1980) emphasize how little is written in the psychological literature on arson-for-profit, 'presumably because it is considered a rational act'.

'For example, an entrepreneur in order to realise rapid economic gains or to support an expensive life-style, may engage in poor business practices and make very risky investments. Because of these activities, his business may do poorly, and as a result he sets fire to his business to collect insurance. The factors which influence his poor business practices and expensive life-style may therefore be more significant than the immediate economic incentives in explaining why he set fire to his place of business . . . This is an area which needs a great deal more research . . .'

Summary

A poor work record is prominent in the studies in the medical literature. Job dissatisfaction, whether through monotony of work, lack of recognition, or other resentment, is a common motive for arson; boredom is a similar motive among the unemployed. 'Grudge' and boredom are thus motives frequently sought for by fire investigators, and no profession is exempt from hazard. The majority of arsonists are undetected, however.

SEXUAL AND MARITAL HISTORY

Sex is an interesting topic. Lewis & Yarnell (1951) devoted 20 pages of their monograph to the consideration of 40 sexually motivated arsonists (who constituted 3.5 per cent of their total sample), but only 29 pages to the study of 200 female fire-setters. Of that which is written about the 'sexual root of arson' (Stekel, 1924), Freud's imagery (1932) must be the most vivid and memorable: 'The warmth radiated by fire evokes the same kind of glow as accompanies the state of sexual excitation, and the form and motion of the flame suggest the phallus in action'.

Whether due to the power of poetry or the natural interest of sex, Lewis & Yarnell's explanatory comments on fire fetishists have been somewhat neglected: 'It is commonly believed that the fire-setter makes the fires for the purpose of stimulating an orgasm, or at least for a substitutive sexual act so that he may feel an equivalent thrill from watching the flames. However, the averge fire-setter is little conscious of such relationship . . . Fire-setting may be considered as a form of substitutive perversion, but the majority of offenders employ it as a temporary indulgence only . . .' Modern authors, surveying their cohorts and finding few sexually motivated arsonists, tend to be rather apologetic. Koson & Dvoskin (1982) for example, muse: 'One must wonder where the "classic" sexually motivated arsonist has gone'.

Fire fetishists almost certainly do exist. Fire investigators take photographs of crowds at fires and recognize the faces of those who are frequent attenders, evincing pleasurable sensations. McGuire *et al.* (1965) provide a useful hypothesis of how a fire 'experience' could become a fire 'fetish', pointing out that a fire fantasy—whether imagined or a recollection of a real event—occurring just before orgasm, is conditioned by the positive feedback of orgasm to become more and more exciting. However, what aspects of fire-setting might be sexually arousing remains entirely unclear. Quinsey *et al.* (1989) found difficulty in selecting the possible various cues for a penile plethysmographic study involving arsonists and volunteer controls listening to audiotaped scenarios, all of which contained some reference to some aspect of fire, apart from the control audiotapes which described 'neutral' activity (a shopping trip) and heterosexual activity. The erectile responses of the arsonists were no different from those of volunteer controls. Both groups showed a greater penile response to the heterosexual scenario, and the scenario describing sexual excitement at a fire. The one subject reported by police to have been masturbating in front of a burning fire, however, showed no penile reponses to any of the fire stories, leaving the issue undecided.

As to the question 'where have all the fire fetishists gone?' the answer can only be speculative. It is possible that some are serving life sentences for arson, since Sapsford *et al.* (1978) noted that there was a high correlation among arsonists in British prisons ($p < 0.005$) between a 'life' (as distinct from a determinate) sentence for arson, and the label 'ever been diagnosed sexually abnormal'. Hurley & Monohan in 1969 described 6 per cent of their Grendon sample as masturbating at fires, and Le Couteur in 1966 noted the erotic motive as frequent in Special Hospital patients. It does not appear, however, that they are currently being referred for a psychiatric opinion.

What then remains to be defined is the degree to which motiveless arson can be attributed to sex, whether as a 'substitutive perversion' or a 'temporary indulgence', among arsonists who are unaware of any such connection. An analyst, Gold (1962), puts the topic into perspective: 'Quite obviously, it isn't just sexual tension alone which has become blocked from normal release that drives people to set fires. If this were the case, no city would be left standing'. Unfortunately modern scepticism about the 'sexual root of arson' has not percolated through to those most directly involved with fire. For example, Barracato (1979), a well-respected fire investigator, in his advice to would-be arson investigators, suggests that in the course of other procedures, they escort and observe the arson suspect while in the bathroom because 'urination is a psychological form of sexual gratification for the pyromaniac, and it's impossible for him to function in front of other people . . .'

Perhaps it is fair to note that themes and motives ebb and flow like fashions, and that if sex was a major preoccupation at the beginning of this century, it has now been replaced with violence and aggression. On that subject, all that can be said with any certainty is that among arsonists who are referred for a psychiatric opinion there is a noticeable dearth of rewarding heterosexual relationships. Where a control population is included, however, there does not appear to be a sufficiently marked difference to suggest that sex is anything more than a contributory factor in the aetiology of arson. Amongst women, who appear proportionately more disturbed, the degree of sexual and marital maladjustment is even greater. However, the sexual and marital status of the vast majority of arsonists is, of course, unknown.

Hurley & Monohan (1969): As one expects with a sample of recidivist offenders, there is poor marital adjustment, social relationships with the opposite sex are difficult, and there is a high incidence of specifically sexual maladjustment . . . This incidence is not markedly different from that for other offence groups. Tennent *et al.* (1971): In general female arsonists appeared to have more problems related to their sexual relationships than the control group, and this was supported by expressed attitudes on sexual problems. Virkkunen (1974): Only 27 per cent of schizophrenic and 40 per cent of control arsonists were married. Hill *et al.* (1982): No difference in the marital status of arsonists, property, and assaultive offenders. Bradford (1982): No significant difference between arsonists and controls. Koson & Dvoskin (1982): Only 11 per cent were married, 89 per cent being divorced, separated, or single (a sexual motive definitely excluded in the majority of the sample). Yesavage *et al.* (1983): 85 per cent of mentally ill arsonists and 48 per cent of non-mentally ill arsonists were single. Harmon *et al.* (1985): Only 7 per cent of women were married at the time of their arrest. O'Sullivan & Kelleher (1987): 70 per cent of both prison and hospital fire-setters were single.

Summary

The 'sexual root of arson', an early theme in the literature, is currently replaced by aggressive themes in the aetiology of arson: modern studies do not find erotic pleasure a motive for arson, although the notion dies hard. Since fire fetishists probably exist, it is possible that they are in prison, since they do not appear to be under psychiatric care. Psychiatric studies reveal a dearth of rewarding heterosexual relationships, but arsonists are probably no different from offender controls in this respect.

PAST MEDICAL HISTORY

Lewis & Yarnell (1951) were undoubtedly influential in exonerating epileptics from an undue burden of criminality, particularly as far as arson was concerned. However, the picture they paint of the medical health of their cohort of arsonists in general has a curiously archaic quality, and it is to be suspected that the criminal has been perceived with the 'halo effect' of his crime. 'We find that the physical configuration plays an important part in the psychological problems of these fire-setters as a group. Again this is often a vague finding which cannot be statistically evaluated, but such observations as "he is grotesquely large", "he is small and feminine in build", . . . "for the first few years of his life he was irritable, a feeding problem and underweight" are prevalent, and with the older offenders we often find that they seem to be falling apart physically . . . In some manner their physical development is atypical and this seems to be one of the most important aetiological factors'.

Certainly there are modern and individual case reports of 'interesting' arsonists, such as 'An XYY man' (Cowen & Mullen, 1979) and 'Arson and Moebius syndrome' (Woolf, 1977), for example. Whether the opinions of Lewis & Yarnell were still unconsciously tainted with the notion of crime as a manifestation of 'hereditary degeneracy' or whether present-day physicians have diminished aesthetic sensibilities, conspicuous ill health and physical abnormality are not prominent features in modern studies of arsonists. Nor would there appear to be anything significant in the physiognomy of that notorious incendiarist of York Minster, Jonathan Martin, whose portrait is shown in Fig. 2.2. Rather, these case reports appear as a reminder of the treatability of certain medical conditions, such as Klinefelter syndrome (Kaler *et al.*, 1989), or the emergence of fire-setting among patients with new illnesses such as AIDS (Cohen *et al.*, 1990).

Fig. 2.2. Portrait of Jonathan Martin. [From A. Morison (1840). *The Physiognomy of Mental Disease*. Published by the author, London.]

Disorders of menstruation

To the mind of nineteenth-century physicians, there appeared to be a clear connection between female crime and disorders of menstruation. Bucknill & Tuke, for example, writing in 1879 on pyromania, had noted: '. . . It is important to ascertain whether signs were present, before the incendiary act, of approaching menstruation, its derangement or suppression . . .' Menstrual problems were not uncommon as a defence in court, as indeed they have been recently, for example, in charges of murder reduced to manslaughter (d'Orban, 1983).

If crime is related to the menstrual cycle, it is most probably related to the premenstrual syndrome, whose best known protagonist, Katharina Dalton (1961) examined newly convicted female prisoners, and found that 49 per cent of them had offended during the paramenstruum, which would have occurred in only 29 per cent of cases on a random basis. The predominant offence in this series was theft, the foremost crime of both men and women. Dalton was particularly concerned about the prevalence of 'premenstrual tension' as distinct from painful menstruation, which she noted was uncommon (14 per cent) among women who committed their crimes during the paramenstruum. Among women convicted for prostitution however, Dalton felt that the incidence of premenstrual tension was probably below that for women in general.

The two main studies of female arsonists have not addressed the question of premenstrual tension. Tennent *et al.* (1971), however, comparing arsonists and controls in Special Hospitals found that significantly more arsonists ($p < 0.01$) suffered from dysmenorrhoea, and a quite considerably larger proportion of them ($p < 0.001$) were thought to be promiscuous, or had convictions for prostitution ($p < 0.01$). The Harmon *et al.* (1985) study reported only a fairly predictable level of gynaecological problems, though it also noted a past history of prostitution in a small proportion of the women.

Confining themselves to violent crime among women, d'Orban & Dalton (1980) included seven arsonists among a series of 50 women charged with violent crime. They found that a significantly higher proportion (44 per cent) had offended during the paramenstruum than could have been accounted for by chance. In discussing the reasons for this relationship, they rejected the view that women are more liable to detection in the paramenstruum, and also the 'social learning theory' of Ellis & Austin (1971) that women may have learned that aggression is more likely to be condoned, particularly in the courts, during this period. Nor did it seem likely that the temporal relationship was fortuitous and depended upon psychological stress either delaying or precipitating menstruation. Rather, it appeared that the 'psychological effects of menstruation may act as a triggering factor to aggressive behaviour in some women who also show evidence of emotional instability at other times', and concluded that 'perhaps too much emphasis has been placed on premenstrual tension symptoms as an aetiological factor in female crime; it is cyclically recurrent, observed behavioural changes (of which the woman herself may be unaware) rather than subjective symptoms which should be looked for, as some may benefit from progesterone or other forms of specific therapy'.

Dalton (1980) reported the apparently successful treatment of three women, charged with offences such as manslaughter, but all of whom, however, had also committed arson amongst many other antisocial and self-injurious acts, with injections of natural progesterone. She recorded that these disruptive behaviours had begun during the year after the menarche, and all the women had previously experienced, certainly superficially, a happy, secure family background with no history of crime. In summary, it would appear, therefore, that a few women committing arson may be helped medically for menstrual disorders, but whether there is any significant association between the crime and either dysmenorrhoea or premenstrual tension, remains unclear.

Summary

Lewis & Yarnell (1951) were influential in exonerating epileptics from an excess of responsibility for arson but considered poor medical health in general as important in the aetiology. Modern studies have not replicated this finding. Disorders of menstruation were considered aetiologically important in arson among women in the nineteenth century but it is uncertain from modern studies whether there is any significant association, or indeed what, if any, significance should be attached to the syndrome of 'premenstrual tension'. Individual case reports emphasize that individual arsonists may suffer from specific, medically treatable, conditions.

HISTORY OF CRIMINAL CONVICTIONS

Two main aspects of the forensic history have been of interest in studies of arsonists; first, the nature of the offence, and whether it throws light on the character and motivation of the arsonist; and second, the issue of potential future dangerousness: that is, the

Table 2.1. *Notifiable offences recorded by the Police, 1989*

Offence	Number of offences (rounded)
Theft and handling stolen goods	2 012 000
Burglary	825 000
Total criminal damage	630 000
Total violence against the person	177 000

chances of re-offending. On both matters knowledge is far from complete.

At the outset it should perhaps be stated that there are some high statistical probabilities about crime in Britain, which are most simply illustrated in Table 2.1, by quoting from recent Criminal Statistics (1989).

Of serious notifiable offences recorded by the Police, two million were for theft or handling stolen goods; some 800 000 offences of burglary were also recorded. In contrast, offences of serious violence against the person numbered approximately 180 000. Put briefly, there are high odds that any arsonist with a previous record has a conviction for an acquisitive property offence.

Concerning the nature of arson, an obvious statement should be made: although usually involving property rather than the person, it is a destructive rather than acquisitive offence. Such offences are also relatively common; of the order of half a million were recorded under the Criminal Damage Act in 1989. Since destruction of property by definition contains an element of aggression, it would be surprising if a proportion of arsonists did not extend their violence against property to violence against the person.

Lewis & Yarnell (1951) found that, despite the 'traditional view of the "firebug" as an inoffensive individual, who,—even if possibly a "degenerate"—with "low mentality" . . . and barred as "yellow" by his fellow criminals—wishes to be a good citizen and criminal activity is contrary to his character', half their cases had been in trouble for one or many other types of antisocial activity, ranging from petty stealing to manslaughter. From subsequent studies it is impossible to say how frequently the entity of the 'pure' arsonist occurs. Studies involving child fire-setters show a high proportion who also demonstrate other types of delinquent behaviour, although there is a small but consistent group who exhibit neurotic symptoms only.

Amongst adult arsonists reported in the literature there would appear to be a trend towards a somewhat higher than chance incidence of violent offences, particularly among women; this is, however, a not unlikely consequence of drawing the offender sample from the 'safe' environment of prison or Special Hospital. But in general, it may be said that although arsonists like most other criminals do not appear to be physically violent, a small proportion of them will demonstrate other forms of dangerously aggressive behaviour. Given below is evidence of criminal and antisocial activity among adult and child fire-setters as it appears in the literature.

McKerracher & Dacre (1966): comparing arsonists and non-arsonists found the records of arsonists to contain rather more aggression to property, rather less interpersonal aggression, and roughly equal acquisitive property offences. Hurley & Monohan (1969): Grendon arsonists were similar in terms of aggressive offences, but had fewer overall property offences than controls; apart from larceny however which most arsonists had in common, they tended to specialize in their other recidivist offences. Tennent *et al.* (1971): study of female arsonists in Special Hospitals had significantly more damage to property ($p < 0.01$) in their histories than controls, and controls significantly more physical aggression to others, but nevertheless 32 per cent of the arsonists had a significant history of physical aggression. Hill *et al.* (1982) in a study comparing arsonists with 'pure' property offenders and violent offenders found that arsonists could be considered a mixture of property offenders and assaultive offenders, with the majority aligning with property offenders. Harmon *et al.* (1985): study of female arsonists, 52 per cent had previous arrest records, of which 33 per cent were for assault.

Studies in children

In Yarnell's (1940) study, the younger group, aged 6—8, were referred primarily for other antisocial activity, such as destructiveness, stealing, running away from home, and truancy. The older group were referred mainly for fire-setting, though a proportion showed marked delinquent trends. Strachan (1981) studying a group of fire-setters at juvenile courts found previous theft: 69 per cent, breaking and entry: 48 per cent, truancy: 30 per cent, and malicious damage other than fire-setting: 23 per cent. Stewart & Culver (1982): 23 per cent were referred primarily for fire-setting, 76 per cent had a referral mainly for fighting, resistance to discipline, disruptive behaviour in school, and stealing. Kuhnley *et al.* (1982) found other delinquent behaviours significantly associated with fire-setters, as compared to non-fire-setters. Heath *et al.* (1983): 31 per cent brought for fire-setting specifically, 69 per cent for other out-of-control problems. Kosky & Silburn (1984): fire-setters were a more conduct-disordered group than non-fire-setters ($p < 0.001$). Kolko & Kazdin (1985): 42 per cent had a primary diagnosis of conduct disorder, and fire-setters evinced greater delinquency, aggressiveness, cruelty, and hyperactivity than non-fire-setting peers. Jacobson (1985b): a diagnosis of conduct disorder described 73 per cent of fire-setters, significantly different ($p < 0.001$) from non-fire-setters.

Arson recidivism

What then is the likelihood of arson being repeated? Three studies have so far undertaken the follow-up of convicted arsonists to determine how frequently they are again before the court. Soothill & Pope (1973) reviewed the subsequent criminal careers of 82 people charged with arson and appearing before the Higher Courts of England and Wales in 1951. Of the eight people in their study who were acquitted of the charge, one subsequently served prison sentences for arson on several occasions.

Of the remaining 75 defendants whom the Court found guilty in 1951, only two had previous convictions for arson. One, described as an 'ex-psychiatric patient of low-grade intelligence' appeared to have abandoned crime altogether after his 1951 conviction, in that he had no subsequent court appearances up to the end of 1971. The second man, however, recorded as 'one of life's unfortunates', subsequently served two substantial prison sentences for arson. These two cases are mentioned because, in the light of present knowledge, the fact of a previous conviction for arson is about the only prognostic factor indicating a likely repetition of the offence.

In contrast to the beliefs widely held in 1973—that arson was an extremely serious untreatable offence, whose perpetrators should be incarcerated for long periods, Soothill & Pope's findings were that only three (4 per cent) of those convicted (for whom they could obtain complete records) were reconvicted of arson in the following 20 years, and they thus concluded that a conviction for arson was very unlikely to recur, but that in follow-up, a very long period should elapse before this statement could be made with safety. Their conclusions are, of course, open to speculation since arson is renowned for its difficulty of detection and for the prosecution's difficulty in gaining a conviction. Given the fact, however, that a large proportion of known fire-setters are young and that a considerable number of offences are thought insufficiently serious to warrant more than a caution, it would appear that arson is an offence with a low likelihood of repetition.

The subjects of Soothill & Pope's study demonstrated the heterogeneous nature of arsonists, ranging in age from 15 to 73 years. For a little under a third of them, the conviction for arson in 1951 was the only conviction ever recorded against them, and only 40 per cent were considered serious enough to warrant a prison sentence.

In the second of these follow-up studies Sapsford *et al.* (1978) in the main concurred that the large majority of men convicted of arson were unlikely to commit it again, and that arsonists as a whole were very similar in their re-offending to any other kind of offender, and certainly no more dangerous to the general public. In contrast to Soothill & Pope, however, Sapsford *et al.* were studying men sentenced to prolonged periods of imprisonment, from life—a practice instituted by the courts since 1964—down to 18 months. The study followed the reconvictions of men for 5 years after release from prison, having served determinate sentences, and also analysed the factors which appeared to have determined the length of sentence.

Three factors appeared decisive in producing a heavy sentence for the offence (i.e., a sentence of 5 years or more, as distinct from a life sentence) and these were: the presence of a criminal history of arson; the absence of any relationship with the victim; and the financial value of the damage. Although the numbers are small for the follow-up period, the reconvictions for arson are quite strikingly different among those sentenced to light and heavy periods of imprisonment. Similar to the figures from the Soothill study, only 2 per cent of 48 cases who had received light sentences had been reconvicted after 5 years. In contrast, however, 20 per cent of the ten cases who had received heavy sentences had been reconvicted for arson after 5 years.

In a third study, Inciardi (1970), an ex-parole officer with the New York State Parole Board, followed the re-arrests for arson of 138 men on parole for the offence over a period of 5 years. The commonest type of arsonist (58 per cent) in his study was 'the wandering hobo', committing arson for 'revenge'. Inciardi does not give figures for re-arrests, noting only in most categories that they were very rare. Even among the 'wandering hobos', only ten out of 80 (12.5 per cent) had long histories of arson recidivism, and amongst these, violation of parole because of arson offences was also very uncommon. His group labelled 'institutionalization' was a small one (6.5 per cent), consisting of residents of 'an institution for mental defectives', who 'had grievances against the institution, and had learned that setting fires would get them transferred to another institution'; they also were re-arrested for arson while on parole, but again, rarely.

Amongst fire-setters in the medical literature, relatively few have had previous convictions for arson—on average 10 per cent—but a considerable number had asked for other offences to be taken into consideration, and, as Koson & Dvoskin (1982) noted, they appear to represent an underprosecuted group. The figures are given below. On the problem of psychiatric patients who set fires there is at present a lack of guidance. Lewis & Yarnell observed: 'It has to be stressed that once a fire has been made, thus breaking through the original inhibition, identical fires may follow until the ''impulse'' is checked by external influences'. Whether such 'external influences' should include charging patients with a criminal offence is open to debate.

Lewis & Yarnell (1951): 30 per cent of 'intelligent' offenders aged 16—20 repeated the offence. Hurley & Monohan (1969): only 10 per cent had previous convictions for arson, although at sentencing 46 per cent had evidently asked for a considerable number of other offences to be taken into consideration; nevertheless 54 per cent appeared to have committed only one offence of arson. Amonst Tennent *et al.* (1971) series of female arsonists, only 47 per cent had ever been prosecuted for arson although 79 per cent had set two or more fires. Molnar *et al.* (1984) series showed that only 7 per cent of partner and 8 per cent of solo arsonists had previous arrests for arson although 58 and 79 per cent of them respectively had criminal records. Hill *et al.* (1982): 29 per cent of cases had a previous record. In Harmon *et al.* (1985) series of female arsonists, only 11 per cent had previous arson charges, although 52 per cent had a previous arrest record. In O'Sullivan & Kelleher's (1987) study of prisoners and patients, 35 per cent had been involved in more than one episode of fire-setting, with recurrences after periods between 6 months and 10 years.

What, if any, conclusions about arson recidivism can be drawn from these studies? Sapsford *et al.* (1978) suggested that a previous conviction for arson is the one factor which indicates the likelihood that it will be repeated with the highest probability, and in this, of course, arson is no different from any other crime. In addition, however, from this study it also appeared that a long prison sentence of 5 years or more increased the statistical probability of repetition, a surprising finding whose validity awaits verification.

As a third factor, Sapsford *et al.* found that the length of sentence actually served, rather than the sentence originally awarded, was a predictor of re-offending. Release on parole is based partly on the prediction score used by the Parole Unit (Nuttall *et al.*, 1977). This prediction score comprises 17 factors which include, for example, the value of property stolen/damaged, number of associates, marital status, living arrangements, and employment position. On a considerable number of these factors the 'typical' arsonist from the medical literature would appear to score with a high likelihood of repetition. Since the majority of arsonists in the study of Sapsford *et al.* did not commit further arson within the follow-up period, it might be inferred that an ordinary prison population of arsonists is quite different from that described by Hurley & Monohan (1969) at Grendon: or that the very presence of adverse prediction factors on the parole score is in itself evidence that arson is a crime with a low rate of recidivism: or, more safely, that too little is known of arson to make accurate predictions, particularly in view of its low rate of detection and conviction.

Summary

In considering the Criminal Statistics in general, acquisitive property offences are extremely common, destructive property offences (Criminal Damage) are fairly common, and offences of violence against the person are relatively rare. Arsonists in the literature are noted to have previous convictions. Their previous convictions do not however, appear to diverge statistically from the norm of general Criminal Statistics sufficiently to shed light on the character of the adult arsonist. Child fire-setters are usually categorized under the heading of 'Conduct Disorder' and thus show other features of delinquent behaviour.

There are few studies of arson recidivism, which is important in assessing future dangerousness. A previous conviction for arson is the most likely predictor that it will occur again. Soothill & Pope (1973) found that a repetition of the offence was very unlikely but that a long period of time should elapse before this could be said with certainty. Sapsford *et al.* (1978) found that the offence was quite often repeated after a long prison sentence had been served for arson; the reasons for this discrepant finding are unknown. Both studies should, however, be viewed with the knowledge that arson is notorious not only for its difficulty of detection, but also the difficulty of obtaining a conviction in court. Amongst psychiatric cohorts a further source of confusion is the notable percentage who have set fires, but have never been prosecuted for the offence, thus never entering the official Criminal Statistics.

ENURESIS, FIRE-SETTING, AND CRUELTY TO ANIMALS

This 'Triad, predictive of adult crime' entered the literature in 1966, since when it has acquired a mythical though increasingly dubious status. Hellman & Blackman (1966), alarmed at a 'tendency to explosive aggressiveness of increasing intensity in our rapidly expanding urban society', examined the childhood history of 84 patients referred from the courts, and concluded that the combination of enuresis, fire-setting, and cruelty to animals in the past history was significantly associated with a current violent, aggressive crime, as distinct from non-aggressive crime.

The precise origin of this slightly curious assembly of symptoms is obscure. Savage (1881), no doubt among many others, had observed the behaviour of the 'morally insane child', amongst whom some 'take to cruelty, and become not only bullies but unmitigated brutes, torturing anything in their power, beginning with the smaller animals and birds . . . This last type of boy not uncommonly develops further —into the masturbator and in this capacity works endless harm in schools . . . In some cases I have seen the children develop so called pyromania'.

It was, of course, the observations of Freud (1932) on the significance of behaviour in terms of its meaning for the stage of unconscious libidinal development reached by the child, that led the way to its psychodynamic interpretation. In 1905, he had noted that it was common to warn children that playing with fire would lead them to wet the bed, and he hypothesized that the appearance of bedwetting in a child was most frequently due to a prohibition against masturbation. In essence, bedwetting indicated that the child was still riveted at the phallic-urethral stage by failing 'to renounce his homosexually based desire to extinguish fire by a stream of urine'.

Klein (1932) had advanced the 'urethral' and 'oral' sadistic components of urination in a child's fantasies of destruction by flooding, drowning, and poisoning; and Fenichel later (1945) had hypothesized that fire-setting was the expression of a sadistic drive seeking to destroy the loved object. Far from being chalk and cheese, fire and water could thus both be seen as symbols of sadistic and aggressive instincts in the child, rebelliously drowning the hostile parent, as he wet the bed at night.

Against this background of psychoanalytic interpretation, Yarnell (1940) had specifically noted that enuresis was present in only nine of the 60 children in her fire-setting study, remarking that it 'seemed a part of the general picture rather than specifically associated with the fire motif'. Michaels & Steinberg (1952), however, were impressed by the persistence of enuresis beyond the age of 15 in young delinquents. Into their study they dropped the fact that 15.8 per cent of these enuretic delinquents had committed recurring acts of arson, in comparison with only 4.9 per cent of non-enuretic delinquents. The particularly aggressive nature of the association was taken up by MacDonald (1963). In his study of 100 patients who had been hospitalized for making threats to kill, two of the patients did go on to kill. It was MacDonald's 'clinical impression' that the unfavourable prognostic factors for a subsequent murder among those who had threatened homicide included: a history of great parental brutality, extreme maternal seduction, paranoid delusions with very great anger, or the triad of childhood fire-setting, cruelty to animals, and enuresis.

It was in this historical context, therefore, that Hellman & Blackman postulated the triad as predictive of violent antisocial behaviour. The theme was taken up by Wax & Haddox (1974), in a descriptive study of six extremely disturbed and assaultive adolescents, in whom, however, the triad, in brief, was not predictive: it was still present, amidst the host of other current disorders of behaviour present in these boys. In the same year, Justice *et al.* (1974) published an account of eight similarly disturbed youths, who, in contrast, did not show evidence of the triad. The major part of their study involved a review of the literature and tape-recorded interviews (779 of them) with people in 25 professions having contact with troubled youth. The clinical impression which emerged from these interviews was that the triad appeared less significant in predicting future violence than a quartet of other behaviours. The debate nevertheless continued, and in 1979 Felthous & Bernard purported to find significance in the fact that from a large series of patients—464—86 had a record of serious assaults, and of these eight (less than 10 per cent) had a past history of two of the signs of the triad. (None of the patients had the full triad.)

If the evidence of Felthous & Bernard was insufficient to dispel the myth of this triad as an especial predictor of violent behaviour, a subsequent study by Heller *et al.* (1984) should certainly do so. Court reports on 1525 offenders who were examined for the presence of the triad and evaluated against crimes of violence (murder, rape, aggravated assault, robbery, assault, or arson) and non-violent crimes, revealed no difference between the violent and the non-violent offenders. 1.2 per cent of violent offenders and 0.5 per cent of non-violent offenders had the full triad of symptoms in their past history; the presence of a partial triad was noted in 17.3 and 15.0 per cent of the two groups respectively. Only cruelty to animals significantly differentiated between those charged with a violent crime and those charged with a non-violent crime (4.3 and 1.3 per cent, $p < 0.01$). In fairness to Hellman & Blackman, it should perhaps be said that the central tenet of their argument, that a child or adolescent demonstrating enuresis and fire-setting and cruelty to animals is seriously troubled and should alert those responsible to active intervention, would not be doubted, and has probably been of considerable value in encouraging such intervention. However, their hypothesis of a particular predictive ability can no longer be accepted.

Summary

This is a triad of childhood behaviours, suggested to be predictive of adult violent crime by Hellman & Blackman (1966). An attempt has been made to trace the emergence of the triad historically, beginning with psychodynamic interpretations of bedwetting and fire-setting, leading to studies demonstrating the persistence of enuresis into adolescence, and its association with delinquency, and MacDonald's (1963) 'clinical impression' that the triad was a poor prognostic factor for an eventual killing among those who had made threats to kill.

Studies of the triad following Hellman & Blackman's work are recorded, and the conclusion reached that there is no particular predictive ability to the triad, although it is still a sign of a seriously troubled child.

INCIDENCE OF MENTAL ILLNESS AMONG ARSONISTS

Arsonists appear on the whole very unlikely to be mentally ill. In trying to define the motives for arson in schizophrenia, Virkkunen (1974) for example, had to search the records of the Helsinki Psychiatric Clinic as far back as 1918 in order to produce a series of 30 patients. Similarly, Yesavage *et al.* (1983) in a French survey, where all arsonists receive psychiatric investigation, needed to include patients committed in 1962 to find 27 mentally ill arsonists for comparison with a straightforward criminal population, and of the mentally ill, 46 per cent were mentally retarded.

The British Criminal Statistics for 1984 revealed that of the 3730 people either convicted of arson or cautioned for it in that year, only 70 received Hospital Orders from the Courts, and of these, only 40 were Hospital Orders with restrictions on discharge; thus of the cases of arson which were cleared up in England and Wales in 1984, only two out of every hundred were committed by people who were suffering from a mental disorder as defined by the Mental Health Act, 1983. Amongst these patients, the diagnosis made was mental illness, as distinct from psychopathy or subnormality, in three-quarters.

Considering the overall extent of crime—some three million offences were then notified annually by the police, in contrast to eighteen thousand recorded offences of arson—and the overall number of Hospital Orders made by the Courts—about 900 that year—arsonists received a disproportionate number of the Hospital Orders: approximately 7 per cent. Similarly, amongst patients detained under the Mental Health Act with special restrictions on discharge, arsonists were over-represented. In 1983, of the total of 1780 an eighth (241) of the patients detained subject to special restrictions had been committed for arson; the figures are interestingly similar to those detained under special restrictions for sexual offences at that time, of which the total figure was 237 patients. That a quarter of the 'criminally insane' were detained for offences of sex and arson must contribute in large part to the notion that these offences are prerogatives of the mentally ill.

An estimate of the prevalence of mental illness based on Criminal Statistics and numbers of Hospital Orders is, of course, extremely crude and overlooks many factors, not the least of which is the current tendency to avoid making medical recommendations to Courts unless there is a high probability that the patient is treatable. Sparse as it is, however, there is a little statistical evidence for the rarity of mental illness. Soothill & Pope (1973), charting the disposal of all those charged with arson and appearing in the higher courts of England and Wales in 1951, recorded that 2 per cent had been found unfit to plead and detained during Her Majesty's Pleasure; 5 per cent had been given a Probation Order with a condition of treatment; and 7 per cent had been committed to psychiatric hospital under the Mental Deficiency Act, 1913. Since that period there has been a marked trend away from disposing of the mentally handicapped by means of Hospital Orders (Robertson, 1981).

A second, more recent, study is that of Molnar *et al.* (1984) who examined all the available records of adults arrested for arson in the jurisdiction of western New York over a 3-year period. Using a very simple diagnosis, only 22 out of 225 arrested (10 per cent) were considered 'psychotic' at the time of the offence.

The other studies available in the medical literature demonstrate the fact that the mentally disordered do commit arson, like any other offence, but the actual figures for prevalence which they provide reflect perhaps, no more than the efficiency of courts in detecting and referring the mentally disordered, since the most common reason for requesting a psychiatric report for the court is the existence of a past psychiatric history (Prins, 1976). Routine psychiatric investigation of all arsonists would appear to be an uncommon practice in most countries.

Thus, to quote the figures from the literature, Lewis & Yarnell (1951) found 25 per cent of men and 32 per cent of women mentally ill, amongst whom 12 and 23 per cent respectively were considered schizophrenic. In Fleszar-Szunigajowa's (1969) Polish study the largest categories were schizophrenia (27 per cent) and mental deficiency (19 per cent). Virkkunen (1974), concentrating specifically on arson among schizophrenics, quotes varying rates for schizophrenia among several continental studies. Two Canadian works from 1982 are those of Hill *et al.* who diagnosed psychosis in 16 per cent, neurosis in 9 per cent, personality disorder in 45 per cent, and mentally retarded in 18 per cent; and of Bradford, where the major findings were of psychosis 9 per cent, neurosis (anxiety and depression) 20 per cent, mental retardation 15 per cent, and personality disorder 53 per cent. The main categories of an Arizona study by Koson & Dvoskin (1982) were: schizophrenia 23 per cent, antisocial personality 15 per cent, mental retardation/organic brain syndrome 11 per cent, and alcoholism 23 per cent. Taylor & Gunn (1984): schizophrenia 30 per cent, personality disorder 35 per cent. Apart from Tennent *et al.* (1971) survey of women in Special Hospitals, there is so far only one article devoted specifically to female arsonists: that of Harmon *et al.* (1985), where again, however, the findings followed the same tendency. Personality disorder was diagnosed in 33 per cent of the women and schizophrenia in 26 per cent.

Several trends emerge from these studies. Firstly, although arsonists may incur the whole gamut of psychiatric diagnosis, the preponderant illness appears to be schizophrenia, however critical one may be about the rigorousness of diagnostic criteria; mental retardation is also prominent. Secondly, despite very small numbers, there is a tendency towards a higher rate of mental illness in women charged with arson, in comparison with men. This tendency is consistent with comparative rates of illness in male and female offenders assessed in St Louis and reported by Herjanic *et al.* (1977). The third point of note is the high rate at which the diagnosis 'personality disorder' becomes attached to arsonists. Tennent *et al.* (1971) noted that female arsonists in Special Hospitals were labelled psychopathic more often than other patients, but not statistically significantly more so. Bradford (1982), commenting on this wondered whether there 'might be a tendency to overdiagnose antisocial personality when assessing arsonists'.

A further fact of concern emerges from two recent studies, representing considerable criticism of current psychiatric services. Koson & Dvoskin (1982) state: 'Over half the total sampled had been involved with mental health and social service agencies just prior to their act of fire-setting and either were rejected or lost to follow-up . . . It is difficult adequately to explain the inability or unwillingness of mental health agencies to serve those who were in contact'. In a similar vein, Molnar *et al.* (1984) note: 'It has been our clinical observation that persons with a history of mental illness are far more frequently arrested for arson than the non-mentally disabled. For example, whereas about 20 per cent of the arrested persons who appear in Buffalo City Court in any given month are known to the Forensic Mental Health Service, 63 per cent of persons arrested for arson over a 4 year span in Erie County were known to the service before their arrest. Many of these persons are revolving door patients and are known to one or more mental health agencies in the county other than the Forensic Mental Health Service'. Comparing two populations of fire-setters, prisoners and hospital in-patients, O'Sullivan & Kelleher (1987) noted a considerable overlap between the two populations, many prisoners showing evidence of psychological disturbance, and observed that 'society's method of dealing with them appeared to be haphazard and arbitrary'.

Summary

Arsonists on the whole are not mentally ill: about 2 per hundred arsonists receive a Court Hospital Order each year. However, considering the small number of Hospital Orders that are passed each year, arsonists appear to be over-represented. The major categories of mental disorder are schizophrenia, mental retardation, and personality disorder; doubts are expressed about whether the offence itself leads to a tendency to overdiagnose 'personality disorder'.

Of those arrested for arson, about 10 per cent are mentally ill. Two recent studies have lodged major criticisms of psychiatric services for failing to deliver adequate health care to mentally disordered arsonists who were already known to the mental health agencies.

MENTAL RETARDATION AND SCHOOL PERFORMANCE

It is received wisdom that 'arson is frequently committed by the subnormal person' (Hunter, 1979) and indeed, from the beginning of medical interest in the subject, pyromania was regarded as the crime of the mentally retarded female adolescent. 'Apart from certain types of minor sexual offences, and to a lesser extent the offence of arson', however, 'there is no particular relationship between crime and mental handicap' (Robertson, 1981).

It is very possibly true that there is a special relationship between arson, and sexual offences, and mental handicap. The mentally handicapped do not usually commit crimes such as embezzlement or fraud, which require a degree of constructive planning beyond their capabilities (Power, 1969). Arson is very easy, however; and sexual desires are not diminished by a lack of intelligence. Certainly, such evidence as is available would support a relationship. In the first 22 years from its opening (1864−86) Broadmoor Hospital, for example, received 103 incendiarists, of whom one-third were diagnosed as suffering from 'congenital imbecility' (Baker, 1892). Similarly, more modern series of arsonists referred for psychiatric evaluation have consistently established a substantial proportion as suffering from mental handicap.

Two lines of argument could, however, support the contrary conclusion, namely that there is no special relationship between mental handicap and arson. The first argument centres on the problem of defining mental handicap, and in this context it should be recalled that the first tests of intelligence were not introduced until the end of the nineteenth century when Binet attempted to elucidate in French prisons how great were the contributions to mental retardation from a native defect of intelligence, and how much from a simple lack of opportunity to learn. Studies from the early nineteenth century, before the availability of intelligence testing, may therefore simply be equating retardation with a lack of education.

Modern studies, however, are beset by the fact that there is no simple definition of mental retardation based on intelligence, but that it is a composite of intelligence and social functioning. Parker's (1974) study of committals of offender patients to the Special Hospitals Rampton and Moss Side under the Mental Health Act showed—apart from the fact that 43 per cent of patients had not had their intelligence tested—that of those committed as 'severely subnormal' and 'subnormal', 69 and 54 per cent respectively had IQs well above the normally accepted levels, one subnormal patient scoring above 100 (Craft, 1984). Le Couteur's comments (Fry & Le Couteur, 1966) on arsonists in Broadmoor Hospital are similar: 'Because of the patients' illness and lack of educational opportunities, some of the earlier IQ assessments are thought to have been considerably underestimated'. How many arsonists have been block-labelled as mentally handicapped, having been committed to hospital under the Mental Deficiency Act, 1913, is uncertain.

A second line of argument against a special relationship between subnormality and arson rests on the general implications of 'the Confait Affair' (Price & Caplan, 1977), in which three boys, one of whom had a mental age of 8 and who spent 3 years in Rampton Hospital, were wrongfully convicted of the murder and attempted arson of the homosexual transvestite prostitute Maxwell Confait. While it should be noted in passing that the three boys had a history of setting 'vandalism' type fires, the confessions obtained from them highlight the suggestibility of the mentally handicapped. Provision for this now obtains in the Code of Practice for the Police and Criminal Evidence Act, 1984.

Since the Confait affair, Fire Officers have been very much aware of the hazards of examining the mentally subnormal, a recent textbook recommending, for example: 'It is desirable that at the time of the interview, the interviewing officers should not know too many details relating to the fire in question because the educationally subnormal are often quick to pick up clues from the interviewer's behaviour, and give the answer which they think he wants' (Cooke & Ide, 1985). Only time will tell whether, under the new 'Judges Rules' for obtaining evidence, there continues to be a preponderance of arson among the subnormal.

It is thus not disputed that the mentally retarded commit arson. That this occurs is only too well known, and indeed is one of the common reasons that makes institutional care a necessity, and within institutions, a terrible danger. To quote O'Gorman (1979): 'A mischievous grown-up baby living amongst people who smoke and who enjoys the excitement of flames, the smoke, the destruction, the fire engine, the hoses, and the noise, constitutes the most serious danger faced by those who care for the mentally retarded'. What appears uncertain, however, is whether the mentally handicapped commit arson at a rate greater than their overall prevalence in the general population, that is, somewhere between 2 and 3 per cent.

Arguments on the one hand have suggested that the truly mentally impaired might be more likely to be 'shopped' by their brighter criminal colleagues, caught because they are not so adept at escape, confess whilst in police custody, and convicted because they had less access to legal aid (Craft, 1984). On the other hand (Power, 1969), they tend to be easily led into mischief, less tolerant of stress, and minor frustrations may lead to impulsive behaviour; they also have a relatively low tolerance of alcohol.

Among adult arsonists studied in the medical literature, there is then a consistently high proportion who are poorly educated and low in intelligence, and the figures are given below. Finally, those who are truly mentally retarded (Power, 1969) show no difference in motivation from those of normal intelligence. As regards their prognosis, however, problems may change with age but the majority are much more persistent (Corbett, 1979) and fire-setting amongst the mentally handicapped must therefore be regarded as a very serious problem.

Hurley & Monohan (1969) noted that, although the sample as a whole fell within the normal range of intelligence, and about half the cases scored at the level of the upper 30 per cent of the normal prison population, the school performance of the sample was predictably poor: only 10 per cent had remained at school after the age of 15; 38 per cent had a history of truancy; and 52 per cent had had special schooling of one kind or another. Inciardi (1970) among a cohort of paroled prisoners found the following IQs: under 70: 19 per cent; 70–90: 34 per cent; 90–110: 25 per cent; over 110: 21 per cent. Tennent *et al.* (1971) noted no difference between female arsonists and non-arsonists in Special Hospitals, in terms of their schooling. Bradford (1982) noted that 38 per cent of arsonists in comparison with none of the controls had had less than 7 years of schooling ($p < 0.001$). Almost half of Yesavage *et al.* (1983) series had been to specialized schools, and 22 per cent were unable to read or write. Harmon *et al.* (1985) study of female arsonists showed that employment history correlated fairly predictably with educational background: 22 per cent of women had dropped out of school early, and had never worked; the bulk of the younger women had not completed their education. Hill *et al.* (1982): 60 per cent of arsonists and controls had a history of truancy from school. Koson & Dvoskin (1982) remarked that educational achievement was somewhat low, and the average number of grades completed (including special education) was only 9.7 years. In contrast, however, in the Molnar *et al.* (1984) study of those arrested for arson approximately half had been to Grade School, a third to High School, and a small percentage had been to college.

Amongst children, Lewis & Yarnell's study expressed the view that defective intelligence was particularly important in the aetiology of fire-setting, since 111 out of 238 children were unable to compete in the classroom, and set revenge fires against the school in early adolescence. Recent studies in which fire-setters are compared with controls, however, do not find that there is any significant difference in intelligence. Rather, it may be said that poor performance at school is a good predictor of delinquent behaviour in general, of which fire-setting appears to be no more than one specific symptom. In view of the evidence of recent studies of child fire-setters therefore, the case for a specific association between arson and mental retardation can only be regarded as weakened, if not resting as 'not proven'.

Lewis & Yarnell (1951): 'defective intelligence is not an important factor in pre-adolescent children and borderline intelligence is no great factor until between 10 and 11 when this type of child begins revenge fires against the school . . . After 16 years the incidence of fires set by mental defectives shows a marked increase'. Vandersall & Wiener's (1970) IQ range was 62–112, with an average of 87, but testing was done selectively. Sixty per cent had experienced academic difficulty. Strachan (1981): 30 per cent were recorded as truanting from school. Gruber *et al.* (1981): approximately 30 per cent attended school sporadically; as expected, most of the children were presenting marked behaviour problems in school. Stewart & Culver (1982) mean IQ, 94, SD = 17, range 48–130. Kuhnley *et al.* (1982): there was no difference between fire-setters and non-fire-setters on the basis of intelligence or history of academic failure. Heath *et al.* (1983) found no difference between fire-setters and the general clinic population in competency, need for special classes or repeating a grade. Kosky & Silburn (1984) found 'No association between fire-setting and mental retardation'. Kolko & Kazdin (1985): there was no difference between fire-setters and non-fire-setters in mean IQ, and range was 55–119. Jacobson (1985): specific reading retardation occurred more often in fire-setters (17 per cent) than non-fire-setters, whatever the age range ($p < 0.001$) but fire-setters showed less, and never worse than mild, intellectual impairment.

Summary

Arson is frequently associated with mental retardation, and evidence supporting this association is observed. Alternative evidence, disputing any particular association, is also considered: the lack of any simple definition of mental retardation based purely on IQ, the lack of formal intelligence testing in Special Hospitals; and the presence of a legal criterion of disordered behaviour in the Mental Health Act definition of mental retardation. In addition, there is evidence suggesting that the mentally retarded may be disproportionately detected and arrested for arson. It is concluded that there is no indisputable evidence associating arson with mental retardation, but that the case is 'not proven'. Provision for police interrogation of the mentally retarded under the code of practice for the Police and Criminal Evidence Act, 1984 may alter future statistics.

Among child fire-setters, poor school performance rather than lack of intelligence is evident, and noted to be a feature of delinquency in general. Mental retardation is a poor prognostic factor in arson.

ALCOHOL

There has long been a known association between alcohol and fire-setting. One of the earliest to be classified is that of Jessen (1860), quoted in Bucknill & Tuke (1879). Jessen was careful to distinguish between cases in which, on the one hand there was a more or less decided motive for arson, and those, on the other, in which the act arose out of a 'diseased mental condition', and among the latter group he arranged his cases according to their association with 'Imbecility, Melancholia, Mania, Monomania, Epilepsy, or Dipsomania'. The numerical association of arson and alcohol had already been noted by Beer in 1871 (quoted in Lewis & Yarnell) who in reviewing 800 cases of fire-setting found that 48 per cent had acted under the influence of alcohol, one-half being spasmodic drinkers and one-half chronic drinkers.

With the caveat that alcoholism may well be over-represented because of its tendency to lead to detection and arrest, the following statistics, all from forensic psychiatric cohorts, are given. In all these studies, alcoholism was associated significantly more often with the diagnosis 'not mentally ill' or 'personality disorder'.

Kammerer *et al.* (1967) found that the crime had been committed in 'a state of inebriation' in more than 50 per cent of cases; 14 per cent of Fleszar-Szunigajowa's (1969) series of abnormal arsonists were diagnosed as suffering from alcoholism; 46 per cent in Grendon Underwood Prison had been drinking prior to the offence and 44 per cent were considered to suffer from alcoholism (Hurley & Monohan, 1969). Inciardi (1970) among paroled prisoners noted 55 per cent to be problem drinkers and categorized those who had a drink problem under the following motives: revenge 36 per cent, excitement/vandalism 14 per cent, in association with insurance or other crime 4 per cent, mental retardation 0 per cent. In a very small series, Foust (1979) found four out of ten arsonists to be intoxicated at the time of the crime. Bradford (1982) diagnosed alcoholic psychosis in 6 per cent, alcoholism in 8 per cent, and states that it was significantly associated with arson (without giving the figures) but was seen as a secondary diagnosis; 26 per cent of Hill *et al.* (1982) series had a 'marked' use of alcohol at the time of the offence, and 47 per cent were chronic 'marked' alcohol users ('marked' being the most severe degree of alcohol use); 38 per cent of Koson & Dvoskin's (1982) series were alcohol intoxicated at the time. Yesavage *et al.* (1983) noted two cases of alcoholic dementia amongst their 'mentally ill' group and that 33 per cent of their 'not mentally ill' group had drunk before committing arson, and in Molnar *et al.* (1984) study, 54 per cent of 'solo' arsonists and 40 per cent of those with 'partners' were, at the time intoxicated with drugs or alcohol. Nine out of 17 prisoners and 10 out of 30 patients had taken a substantial quantity of alcohol at the time, in O'Sullivan & Kelleher's (1987) comparative study.

Lewis & Yarnell (1951) remarked that it was among adult males (over the age of 20) that there was an increased association of arson and alcoholism; amongst females, 20 per cent were 'known to have used alcohol to excess'. However, the only recent study of female arsonists, that by Harmon *et al.* (1985), shows the same tendency; 55 per cent of their group had either been alcoholics or heavy drinkers, and 20 per cent were drunk at the time of the offence, reflecting perhaps the increased prevalence of alcoholism among women, or the more aggressive stance currently being taken towards the detection and prosecution of arson, which no longer spares the female.

In discussing the manner of the association between alcohol and arson the approach taken is usually one of '*in vino veritas*', viewing the drug as one with powerful disinhibiting effects which 'by exercising its pernicious influence on the brain tends to weaken the power of self-control in many individuals who might otherwise hold in check their revengeful passions' (Baker, 1892). Thus, among the fathers of psychoanalysis, Freud is quoted as seeing the adult arsonist under the influence of alcohol becoming a child, archaically infantile; Ferenczi, as seeing alcohol as the destroyer of sublimation; and Jung as viewing alcohol as a libido releaser, allowing energy to stream out in false directions, thus relieving the immediate pressure, but causing a psychological regression to a more infantile position (Lewis & Yarnell, 1951).

Kammerer *et al.* (1967), noting in the French literature that arson shares pride of place with sexual offences as the type of crime most strongly associated with alcohol, divided the association into four groups. Firstly, chronic alcoholism with its attendant social decline would accentuate underlying personality traits, bringing feelings of hatred and vengeance nearer to the surface and making them more liable to be acted upon. Secondly, and most frequently, sporadic and acute alcoholic intoxication might intermittently though very danger-ously, liberate primitive drives such as power, sexuality or anger, and lead to fire-setting. Thirdly, though rarely, the subject might set fires either by accident or through delusions in a state of acute alcoholic hallucinosis. Fourthly, in a state of alcoholic dementia, confusion, irritability or misjudgment, alone or in combination, might result in potentially fatal behaviour.

In an attempt to clarify the role of alcohol in states of acute intoxication, Virkkunen (1984) compared two groups of arsonists who were divided by their response to a glucose tolerance test. One group showed reactive hypoglycaemia in response to the test, and as a group their diagnoses were on analysis, antisocial personality, or intermittent explosive personality disorders; they were described as habitually violent when under the influence of alcohol. An estimation of their reasons for arson proved very difficult through lack of any clear conscious motive: fire-setting appeared to be instinctive, impulsive behaviour. Their fires were usually very dramatic, and in some cases they had intended to burn themselves, although, as stated, their motives were chaotic and conflicting. They appeared to have been more or less confused when setting the fires, and in a number of cases had tried to put them out.

In contrast the arsonists with normal glucose tolerance tests appeared to have had much more conscious and premeditated motives for arson, which were typically either revenge or a desire for attention; as a group they were not habitually violent when drunk, although a proportion of them were classified as antisocial personalities.

Virkkunen postulated that the first group, who ate little or nothing during their drinking bouts, were in danger of developing alcohol-induced fasting hypoglycaemia, through the action of alcohol in inhibiting hepatic glucose production, and thus were prone to acting in a state of confusion. This mechanism might help to explain a proportion of some alcohol-related arsons which are repetitive yet apparently motiveless. Virkkunen *et al.* (1989b) in a subsequent study of men reconvicted of arson and other violent offences after their original forensic psychiatric evaluation found that it was possible to predict recidivism with an 84 per cent accuracy on the basis of the abnormal glucose tolerance test and low concentration of 5-hydroxyindoleacetic acid in the cerebrospinal fluid. However, these men had almost invariably reverted to drinking after their release from custody, and there was no explanation, of course, why fire itself was the chosen vehicle of violence.

Alcoholism is a much more important factor in relation to the diagnosis 'personality disorder' than to schizophrenia, where the illness itself often appears sufficient cause for arson. In terms of diagnosis, however, two other associations of alcohol have not yet been elucidated. Firstly, it is of note that depression is a relatively uncommon diagnosis among cohorts of arsonists, and it is therefore possible that alcoholism might be one of its manifestations within the 'depressive spectrum'. Secondly, the classic descriptions of 'the irresistible impulse'—'the mounting tension, the restlessness, the urge for motion, headaches, palpitations, ringing in the ears, and the gradual merging of their identity into a state of unreality' (Lewis & Yarnell)—are highly reminiscent of an anxiety state. It is therefore conceivable that a proportion of arsonists are medicating themselves by using alcohol as an anxiolytic, as is common in other anxiety states.

In the context of recidivism and the assessment of dangerousness, the importance of alcoholism is stressed in relation to the sporadic nature of the 'binge' drinker—in contrast to the chronic alcoholic—whose unpredictable bouts of drinking render him 'conditionally' dangerous. Thus in a proportion of cases, it is the treatability of sporadic alcoholic bouts which is the criterion. Koson & Dvoskin, in their admittedly very small series, noted a further difficulty, namely that the patients were drinking in the context of a situational crisis, the prediction of which could only successfully be determined by very close monitoring.

One final hazard of alcohol, in relation to death by fire rather than to the act of arson, is the finding of Anderson *et al.* (1981). Toxicological analysis of the victims of fire who had died in their own homes in London revealed that 14 per cent of the dead had blood alcohol levels over 150 mg/100 ml, a level which would severely inhibit their capacity to escape. In a survey they had previously conducted, in the Glasgow area, one-quarter of all who had died in fires had a blood alcohol level over 150 mg/100 ml. Whether such findings indicate merely the carelessness of drunken accidents, or unsuspected suicidal tendencies, is, of course, open to speculation.

Summary

Historically, the association of arson with alcohol has long been known, as has its tendency to act as a drug with a powerful disinhibiting effect. The increased likelihood of detection and arrest while in a state of acute intoxication is noted. The mental states induced by alcohol are acute intoxication, chronic alcoholism, hallucinations, and dementia.

More recently, studies have questioned whether there is a tendency to overdiagnose 'personality disorder' in relation to alcoholism, and have raised the possibility of other diagnostic categories, such as a confusional state due to reactive hypoglycaemia in some cases of acute intoxication (Virkkunen, 1984); the possibility of alcoholism as a 'depressive spectrum' disorder and the role of the alcohol as an anxiolytic have not yet been elaborated, nor has its role in relation to death by fire at home.

Alcohol is known to be an important and often unpredictable factor in arson recidivism.

SUICIDE BY FIRE

Bourgeois (1969) begins his article on suicide by fire with a salutary warning taken from the *Annales d'Hygiene*, 1829: 'Les journaux devraient s'abstenir d'annoncer un suicide, quel qu'il soit'. Writing on the same theme in 1896, Henry Maudsley said: 'There can be no doubt that the act of violence . . . is sometimes suggested by the sensational reports of similar deeds in the newspapers. The example is contagious; the idea fastens upon the weak or depressed mind and becomes a sort of fate against which it is unable to contend'.

Western writers find suicide by fire one of the most repugnant forms of death; one of the most violent, rare, and difficult to understand. Bourgeois suggests that we are still too close to the deliberate and barbaric persecutions of heretics in Western civilization through the Middle Ages, to be able to discard our 'sacred horror' of death by fire. He quotes one of the earliest psychiatric textbooks, Falret's 1822 edition of *De l'hypochondrie et du suicide*' in which Falret shares the cultural outrage of the British in India on encountering the tradition of 'suttee': 'Despite the public statement of Lord Binning and the British Government that suttee must stop, 2366 widows publicly burnt themselves to death on their husband's funeral pyre last year (1821) . . . and who knows how many more silently immolated themselves privately within their own homes'. A more modern study by Modan *et al.* (1970), however, provides evidence of persisting ethnic differences in the method of suicide; comparing completed and attempted suicides in Israel in the 2-year period 1962–1963, the authors noted that over three-quarters (77 per cent) of Asian and African-born women who had completed suicide, had killed themselves by fire in comparison with such 'traditional' methods as self-poisoning used by European immigrants. Amongst those attempting suicide, burning was again prominent only in those of Oriental origin, of both sexes. Zemishlany *et al.* (1987), whilst disputing that suicide by burning is common in contemporary Israel, nevertheless reported the contagious effects of three attempted suicides in a psychiatric hospital there.

Barbaric as it no doubt seems, a second line of cultural tradition apart from 'suttee' suggests that death by fire is not quite so alien to human nature as we would no doubt prefer to believe. From the fifth century onwards there are well documented records from both India and China of the training of Buddhist monks perfecting themselves in the art of absolute detachment; the ultimate in training, self-immolation by fire, was not a sign of sacrifice, but a total detachment from the world before the attainment of Nirvana.

It was, of course, through the diversion of this Buddhist religious tradition to political ends, when the Buddhist monk Thich Quang Duc immolated himself by fire in Saigon in 1963 as a political protest against the Diem government and was followed by some 30 other deaths by Buddhist monks over the years until 1967, that suicides by fire became noticeable throughout the Western world. Contributing to this somewhat mythical aura, must have been the death of Jan Palach in 1969 in protest at the Russian invasion of Czechoslovakia.

Prior to the 1960s then, was suicide by fire a rare phenomenon in the West? Continental writers, where, of course, suicide had been decriminalized from a much earlier period than in Britain, felt that it was, and was resorted to only by psychotics and those who had become 'insensible a la douleur'. Davis, however, writing in 1962, before these events had become publicized, described five suicides in Florida, all of whom had died at home by fire and all of whom had experienced definite previous psychiatric problems. Noting that it was a relatively common phenomenon in Cuba, as well as the Middle East, he commented: 'All too frequently, the victim is presumed to have died accidentally, in the absence of an adequate investigation . . . In death involving fire, the psychiatric background of the victim should be carefully evaluated as part of the arson investigation'.

Regarding its incidence, it is, of course, a very dramatic phenomenon, and worthy of newspaper headlines. Though newspaper headlines cannot be regarded as any more reliable than other forms of statistics, Bourgeois (1969) quotes for what they are worth, the numbers referred to in newspapers: between 1957 and 1963, 635 suicides recorded, five of which by fire; from 1963−69, 105 suicides by fire.

A similar epidemic of suicide by fire occurred in Britain between 1978 and 1979 when coroners recorded 82 suicides by fire compared with an average of 23 each year in the preceding 15 years since the Thich Quang Duc event. The British epidemic followed the well-publicized self-immolation of a young female Australian heiress, Lynette Phillips, a convert to a quasi-religious Asian sect, who was making a political protest about the legal detention of her cult leader in India. Miss Phillips, having been deported from Britain after threatening to kill herself in Parliament Square, eventually died in flames in front of the *Palais des Nations* in Geneva.

Ashton & Donnan (1981) who recorded the subsequent suicides and the information known about them from the reports available at the coroner's inquests, entered a plea for a code of restraint in the practice of reporting suicide by the media. They pointed out that, as far as was known, none of the coroner's suicide victims was politically motivated, and that 90 per cent of them had received previous psychiatric treatment; they noted that the epidemic had passed, but that the method of suicide by fire might well permanently have become endemic in Britain at least. In a discussion of the trends in the suicide rate for England and Wales in the years 1975−1980, McLure (1984) noted that there had been an overall rise in the rate of suicide, and that in particular suicide by such violent methods as hanging, strangulation, and suffocation (in both sexes) and suicide by drowning and jumping from a high place (in females) had increased over the period. Since these methods of suicide were not newly available, McClure suggested that they might have been a substitution for decreasingly available methods such as toxic domestic gas. Suicide by fire remained, however, apart from the epidemic recorded by Ashton & Donnan, either unsuspected and unrecognized as Davis had suggested, or at a very small and stable level.

Andreasen & Noyes (1975) in an interesting liaison psychiatry survey of victims in a Burns Unit at the University of Iowa noted, as Ashton & Donnan had done, a similar lack of political motivation among patients on the Unit who were recorded as being both suicidal and burnt. These were 2 per cent of the patients, and their psycho-pathology was remarkable for being severe but not neatly classifiable. The ages of the victims ranged from 16 to 75 years and the diagnoses throughout the spectrum, from porphyria to mental retardation. They noted that a high proportion of the patients were women, but could find no explanation for it. Further exploration by liaison psychiatrists in this field might very well begin to clarify the incidence of suicide by fire. It is quite possible, for example, that at least a small percentage of deaths at home, at present attributed to accident, are the result of depression in alcoholism. The survey of blood alcohol levels in the victims of fire previously referred to showed high blood levels in a significant proportion of the dead (Anderson *et al.*, 1981).

Suicide by fire does not so far appear to have been recorded among children. Nor, surprisingly, is it a method that is at all common in prison, in Britain at least (Topp, 1973, 1979). Within the hospital setting, the subject has so far been investigated only by Jacobson

(1986) whose major finding was that, although unusual, the phenomenon was not rare; in this particular hospital survey the method was more common than all other violent attempts at suicide, apart from self-strangulation. Like the patients from Andreasen & Noyes' series, Jacobson's patients were characterized by severe illness including a history of violent and sometimes bizarre attempts at self-destruction; similarly, there was an over-representation of religious preoccupations, though without the heavy preponderance of females. It was a small series comprising only 12 patients. Four of them, however, had a history of childhood arson, and had burnt themselves with cigarettes which were features not found in the control group and not previously considered indicative of suicidal behaviour (Pao, 1969).

Turning then to the medical literature on arsonists, it is perhaps not surprising to find that there is a small but notable percentage who show either suicidal or self-destructive behaviour.

McKerracher & Dacre (1966): 13 and 23 per cent of arsonists respectively had manifested self-mutilation and attempted suicide, which contrasted with controls at the $p < 0.05$ and < 0.01 levels of significance; all were males; Hurley & Monohan (1969): 26 per cent attempted suicide on one or more occasions; Tennent *et al.* (1971): suicide had been attempted by 51 per cent of arsonists and 59 per cent of controls; self-mutilation had occurred in 51 per cent of arsonists and 39 per cent of controls. Dalton (1980) described three women prisoners with self-destructive behaviour and arson; Hill *et al.* (1982) noted that 44 per cent of arsonists had attempted suicide in the past, but that this did not differ significantly from predominantly 'property' or 'violent' offenders; Molnar *et al.* (1984): motive for arson described as a death-wish in 8 per cent of solo-arsonists. Harmon *et al.* (1985): 7 per cent had attempted suicide. Described in individual cases by Topp (1973) and Boling & Brotman (1975). In the most recent survey O'Sullivan & Kelleher (1987) found that of arsonists in prison, in hospital, and self-immolators, 39 per cent had a history of prior self-mutilation and 51 per cent a record of prior parasuicide.

Depression, in contrast, is a comparatively infrequent diagnosis among forensic psychiatric cohorts for which the figures in the recent studies are as follows: Hurley & Monohan (1969): neurotic depressive reaction: 4 per cent; Tennent *et al.* (1971): 9 per cent; Bradford (1982): 17 per cent, with a higher rate among women (figures not stated); Harmon *et al.* (1985): only one case (4 per cent); O'Sullivan & Kelleher (1987): 13 per cent.

It is quite uncertain what, if any, significance should be attributed to these figures, which might suggest a link between suicide and arson, but which may well indicate no more than the fact that self-destructive acts are a form of manipulative behaviour that is relatively common among those in institutions for any offence. The comparative 'absence' of depression may, alternatively, reinforce the notion of alcoholism as an illness within the depressive spectrum—or simply signify that alcoholism and arson are both common. In addition, the recent finding of Geller & Bertsch (1985), that among in-patients in a psychiatric hospital there was a significant association ($p < 0.05$) between a history of fire-setting and a history of non-lethal self-injurious behaviour, lends food for speculation. The only inference might well be that arson is a far more common and less repetitive activity than has so far been supposed. The matter awaits clarification.

Summary

The concept is noted to be deeply repugnant to Western writers, but to be part of cultural tradition in the East as witnessed by the practice of 'suttee' in the past, and present-day methods of suicide in Israel. It appears to have emerged as a phenomenon in the West following the influence of political suicides during the Diem war and the Russian invasion of Czechoslovakia, and to have reached 'epidemic' proportions in Britain in the year 1978—79. It is suggested that the psychiatric background of the victim should be a routine part of investigations into deaths by fire.

Andreasen & Noyes' (1975) study in a Burns Unit had indicated suicidal intentions in 2 per cent of patients. In the official statistics for this country, despite a rise in the rate of suicide by violent methods over the period 1975—1980, the rate of this particular method remained very small and stable. It is suggested that this method of suicide may be more common than at present recorded; an apparent link between arson and self-destructive acts would also warrant investigation.

1984). Kammerer *et al.* noted that three-quarters of the fires among their group of arsonists were set at the beginning of the evening, in the hours of darkness, at a time when the majority of fires could be expected anyway. Speculating on the reasons, they considered that darkness allows time for escape and a delay in detection; that it is a time for getting drunk, and possibly also the hour for reverie and contemplation. In general then, no inference of intent can therefore be drawn from fires set at 'peak times'.

Emerging from the study of Molnar *et al.* (1984), however, which included all arrested arsonists, was the significant finding that among 'arsons-for-profit' which had been undertaken with a partner, 78 per cent occurred between midnight and 6.00 a.m., and only 5 per cent during the hours of daylight. Fire-investigators are thus very much aware that he who appears fully dressed in the middle of the night at the time of the fire, or indeed he who discovers the fire, is also first in line for suspicion of having set it (Cooke & Ide, 1985).

Though in no sense conclusive, other characteristics of the time can sometimes follow a pattern which may point to the fire-setter. 'Those concerning children' for example (Home Office report, 1990), 'are most prevalent when they are free from constraints of school, i.e., at weekends, during the spring and summer holidays, and otherwise in the late afternoon'. Alternatively, groups of vandals,'often unimaginative creatures of habit' (Cooke & Ide, 1985) often frequent the same areas from week to week, and are particularly active on the nights of Friday, Saturday, and Sunday. Fire-bugs may demonstrate their own idiosyncrasies, by embarking on a binge of minor fires, until the impulse has burnt out over the period of a day, or alternatively setting 20 fires in a week, or 100 fires over several years. One of the possibly least helpful, but not yet replicated analyses of fire statistics, was the Fire Research Station's 1968 report that the seventh day after the new moon represented a time for maximum demands on Fire Brigade activity.

The notion of time, in relation to epidemics of fire-setting, has been observed by Lewis & Yarnell (1951), saying: 'Though not statistically validated, there is an impression that incendiarism does occur in waves, and it appears that Mönkemöller, Schmid and others were right in stating that suggestion and imitation precipitate some fire-setting: juveniles or mental defectives who are looking for a method of antisocial behaviour may get the idea from hearing or reading newspapers or pseudo-detective story accounts of outstanding "fire-bugs"'. Within institutions such as prison or hospitals, such epidemics are described (e.g., Topp, 1973) but rare, as documented by Tardiff (1982) and Zemishlany *et al.* (1987); suggestions as to their management have been made by Boling & Brotman (1975) and Rosenstock *et al.* (1980).

Geller (1984) writing from Massachusetts, in the context of much public disquiet over the 'deinstitutionalization' of psychiatric patients and their alternative accommodation in community placements, noted an increase in rates of admission to hospital for fire-setting over the 'decade of deinstitutionalization' 1972−1982, from six per 1000 to 17 per 1000 admissions to hospital . While Geller's study might be interpreted as a generalized expression of psychiatrists' unease with the very restrictive 'civil libertarian' mental health legislation currently in force in Massachusetts, his observations on 'arson (as) an unforeseen sequela of deinstitutionalization' should perhaps be kept in mind during the period of our own planned closure of large mental hospitals. Geller noted in his study that at least one patient, with no previous history of arson, had witnessed the treatment of another arsonist while in hospital, and had followed the extensive press coverage given to this patient. 'When she herself was subsequently refused readmission to hospital, she resorted to arson. Her lawyer defended her in court by proclaiming: "She only set the fire to get back into hospital"'.

Summary

The times of Fire Brigade attendances are recorded by law. Most domestic fires occur in the second half of the day, when people are most active in their homes. Some inferences may be drawn from the time of the fire: for example, arson for profit may occur in the early hours of the morning, vandalism fires in school holidays, and epidemics of fire-setting may occur in institutions. The American experience of an increase in hospital admissions for fire-setting as a consequence of deinstitutionalization and its implications for our own planned closures of large mental hospitals are noted.

THE SITE OF THE FIRE

In the past arson has been considered a predominantly rural offence, its classic target being the haystack, which, it has to be said, must appear an ideal ready-made bonfire to the *aficionado*. Currently, in Britain at least, certain forms of arson such as vandalism are, in contrast, a besetting problem in inner-city areas, where the usual victim is derelict, neglected, isolated, and ill-lit—vulnerable—public property. In such areas, ready-made bonfires also tend to accrue.

Local studies within individual police sub-divisions have shown that the degree of severity of vandalism generally matches that of cases of deliberate fire-setting. It should perhaps also be noted, that in attempting to assess the reasons for such mindless acts of vandalism, criminological explanations have shifted from psychological reasons —such as aggression and frustration—to more sociological reasons— such as lack of employment, lack of stimulating schooling, and inadequate provision for youngsters 'to express their developmental needs in legitimate ways' (Home Office, 1980). However, in turn also, public victims such as schools are currently being encouraged to take a much more aggressive stance in their own defence, such as reporting and repairing acts of damage, considering the flammability of building materials used, involving the Crime Prevention Officer, the Fire Safety Officer, etc. (Fire Prevention, 144). If the site of the fire in vandalism-arson is in a sense a study in victimology, it is also extremely important in suggesting motivation, both to the fire investigator and to those assessing the motivation of the arsonist once caught.

The study of Sapsford *et al.* (1978) of arsonists in prison noted that those who received long sentences appeared to have done so, in part, because there was little explicable relationship between the arsonist and the victim. It does have to be reiterated, however, that, as very few arsonists are caught, any assumptions made on the basis of what is known from the medical literature could be positively misleading. To the mind of the fire investigator, the psychotic arsonist is one of the most perplexing, for, as Lewis & Yarnell put it, they 'first burn their own homes, often in a suicidal attempt, though the paranoid schizophrenics will burn anything they believe God wants burned'. However, women predominantly, but also a considerable proportion of men remanded for psychiatric reports, appear to set fire to their own property. Fires are often set within a narrow radius of home; often there is an emotional link of malice between the arsonist and the victim, whether as teacher, employer, rejecting spouse or friend: the 'Institution' or authority figure of school or work or hospital are common targets, but the Church today is far less frequently attacked than in former times. Below is given a summary of the property destroyed from the literature.

Hurley & Monohan (1969): the following property was destroyed: dwelling houses 21, barns and haystacks 13, commercial property 24, schools 3, hotels and clubs 3, churches 2, theatres 1. In 50 per cent the property owner was unknown to the defendant; in the other 50 per cent the relationship was as follows: parent, employer, friend, girl-friend/wife, landlord, and doctor. Tennent *et al.* (1971): of the fires set by females in the Special Hospitals, 33 per cent were set in hospital, 24 per cent in their own home, 13 per cent in a relative's or boyfriend's home, 11 per cent in prison or borstal, 3 per cent at work, and 13 per cent 'other', e.g., telephone kiosk, church, or shop. Hill *et al.* (1982): the victim could be identified as an institution/ organization in 39 per cent of fires, and as a person in 19 per cent, with a relationship to the arsonist in the following descending order of frequency: parent, stranger, teacher/school, landlord, employer, wife/girl-friend, relative, friend. Bradford (1982): 60 per cent set a fire within 1 mile of home. Twenty-nine per cent set their own homes alight, 23 per cent set another single dwelling alight, and 26 per cent a multiple storey or apartment dwelling. One individual set fire to a factory. Molnar *et al.* (1984): of solo arsonists, 40 per cent had been set in their own home, 2 per cent in the same building and 7 per cent next door to home; 78 per cent were set within 1 mile from home. Of partner arsonists, only 22 per cent had been set in their own home, in the same building, or next door, and 49 per cent were set more than a mile from home. Harmon *et al.* (1985): of women charged with arson, the fires had been set: 44 per cent in their own home, 15 per cent in a lobby, etc., of their own home; 19 per cent in the home of another, and 14 per cent in lobby, hall, etc., of another; 11 per cent were non-residential.

Summary

The sites of Fire Brigade attendances are recorded by law. Arson is noted to have changed from a predominantly rural to an urban offence, and to occur prominently in vicinities which are otherwise highly vandalized. The possible emotional significance of the property destroyed is important in assessing motivation, and appears also to be significant in determining the sentence for the offence passed by the Courts.

ALONE OR IN PARTNERSHIP

Group fire-setters—described by Lewis & Yarnell (1951) as 'village "hoodlums" setting fires in the course of other asocial depredations' are sparse in cohorts sent for psychiatric evaluation. Numerically and financially they are, however, very important omissions. Lewis & Yarnell observed that, of fire-setters between the ages of 13 and 20, more than twice the number were acting with a partner or a gang than set fires alone. Molnar *et al.* (1984), attempting to overcome some of the distortions inherent in biased sampling, examined all the available records of those arrested for arson in a western New York jurisdiction. Numerically, those acting with one or more partners comprised a third of all those arrested. Just as significantly, however, the presence of a partner appeared to be the one single factor that most effectively discriminated between types of fire-setters.

From the financial aspect, Lewis & Yarnell observe that the young are indifferent to the value of property. In their study no attempt was made to estimate the financial loss involved, but the general observation was made that 'these boys set many more fires than the boys working alone, and they did considerably more damage. In their fires, two people were killed, and two injured, and four firemen were injured; some groups caused damage up to a million dollars . . . .' Molnar *et al.* also observed that those acting with partners caused higher property damage: 48 per cent of those acting with partners had caused damage valued at over $10 000 in comparison with 51 per cent of solo arsonists who, for example, had caused damage valued at under $500. Strachan's (1981) study of fire-setters in a juvenile court similarly noted that 40 per cent of cases had caused damage valued at over £1000, in contrast to cases of 'ordinary criminal damage' which were valued at under £25 in 65 per cent of cases. To overlook gang activity can thus in one sense seriously overestimate the potential hazard of solo arsonists.

Gang activity—the masculine herd instinct—is of course a very normal phenomenon in the turbulent period of male adolescence. The motives for arson in this age group are those of vandalism in general, extending from over-exuberant play, to damage as a proof of toughness, to damage as a palliative to boredom. Ultimately, of course, with a thin admixture of a political or social statement, vandalism becomes riot and terrorism. The simplest example most close to home is that of the Welsh Nationalist extremists whose campaign against the English with holiday homes in their territory was parodied in the phrase: 'Come home to a real fire: buy a holiday cottage in Wales'.

In the study of Molnar *et al.*—a comparison of partner and solo arsonists—37 per cent of arsonists working with partners had motives ascribed to 'vandalism' or 'excitement', in comparison with 16 per cent setting fires on their own; these were adolescents. An equally significant finding in the Molnar study was, however, that among the older arsonists who were arrested, 37 per cent of those with partners were working for profit (in comparison with 3 per cent of solo arsonists). If the overall number of arsonists-for-profit in the

Molnar series is low, it is possibly no more than a reflection of the fact that arson for profit is difficult to detect and arrest.

As to the prediction of future fire-setting activities, Lewis & Yarnell considered group activity as a hopeful prognostic sign, being in most cases no more than a developmental stage, among boys whose individual psychopathology was less severe than those who acted alone. Soothill & Pope (1973) also found that it was younger men who tended to be jointly charged with arson, and noted that none of those jointly charged repeated the offence over the next 20 years. In similar vein, a much higher proportion of solo arsonists in the Molnar study already had previous contact with mental health agencies and had criminal records; none of those arrested with a partner were, in contrast, considered psychotic. Among adult criminals also, the presence of a partner indicates the possession of a certain degree of social skill in interpersonal relations involving the abilities to plan, trust, and execute a course of action (Molnar *et al.*, 1984). In general, then, group activity is a hopeful prognostic factor in arson.

Summary

The study of Molnar *et al.* (1984) demonstrated that the omission of 'group' fire-setter studies has been an important omission both numerically and financially. Between the ages of 13 and 20, fire-setting in groups is twice as common as in isolation; the damage caused by groups tends also to be considerably financially greater. The presence of a partner may, in general, indicate different motivation, less severe psychopathology, and have a better prognosis for recidivism.

4 Psychological motives for arson

As comprehensive a list as possible for the reasons for arson, as detailed by the US Fire Administration (1979), has been given above. In presenting the reasons as they are documented in the medical literature, it should be noted from the outset that the crime-for-profit category, into which many offences of arson would fall, is rarely encountered. One cause for this is that such offenders are rarely referred for a medical report. Another cause, put, for example, by Virkkunen (1974), is that among schizophrenics 'insurance fraud is not a reason for setting fires. This may be accounted for partly by the fact that these offenders seldom possess much personal property. However, the reason for this could also be that their illness makes them unable to carry out anything that requires long calculation'. Putting it in a subtly French manner, Yesavage *et al.* (1983) remark: 'Such crimes are difficult to solve, and are perpetrated by individuals who are more devious and of a higher social class, and thus more likely to avoid conviction'.

Similarly, other common categories of arson such as politically motivated or terrorist activity, featuring almost daily in newspaper headlines and television news reports, are rarely elaborated in textbooks of psychiatry, although they are graphically described in books of more general interest such as those of Barlay (1972), Scott (1974), and MacDonald (1977). Likewise, arson to cover up crime appears uncommonly in the medical literature, since it is considered a purely criminal pursuit and is not routinely referred for a psychiatric opinion apart from such comparatively rare instances as, for example, arson to conceal a murder.

Nevertheless, as Perr (1979) reminds us, crime occurs in a social context, and if the writers of the nineteenth century have left us with the heritage of arson as the offence of the 'mentally retarded female adolescent servant', we should, when assessing psychological aspects of behaviour today, increasingly keep in mind the rapidly changing pattern of society with its portrayal of 'instant riot and arson' that is reflected on our televisions. Nor should we overlook the benefits of our modern society, such as the rapid payments offered by insurance companies; for it might legitimately be wondered how often a chip-pan fire occurs just when a kitchen needs redecoration—or the compensations offered by a welfare state: Perr, writing from New York, suggests that perhaps 10 per cent of fires involve welfare fraud, whether to replace lost furniture, clothing, or appliances; or perhaps even to become top of the council housing list.

In attempting to review the motives for arson as they appear in the literature, the words of Rider (1980), a special agent for the FBI, are appropriate: 'Though much has been written on fire-setting behaviour, the literature provides little practical information for the investigator beyond a multiplicity of diverse and arbitrary classification systems, a variety of motivational factors, and a number of narrowly defined clinical profiles or composites of arsonists'. Rider might well have met with sympathy had he said more simply: 'It all seems rather muddled and confusing'. For the sake of simplicity, an attempt will be made to group them under four categories of aggressive behaviour, as described by Edmunds (1978):

1. Acquisitive—i.e. attacking innocent persons/property for gain.
2. Vindictive—i.e. behaviour aimed at hurting a perceived aggressor.
3. Instrumental—i.e. behaviour designed as a tactic to achieve an end, in response to some environmental stimulus.
4. Cathartic—as an expression of an emotion such as anger or tension or despair, but against a random target.

ACQUISITIVE

(Damage caused in the course of gain.) As already stated, arson-for-profit features very rarely in the medical literature; Lewis & Yarnell (1951) had, for example, specifically excluded this category from their study. Molnar *et al.* (1984): working with a partner 37 per cent, solo arsonists 3 per cent. Prins *et al.* (1985): 17 per cent.

VINDICTIVE

(Damage aimed to cause suffering to a perceived aggressor.)

Revenge

Revenge is one of the motives most commonly cited for arson. One of the best documented and spectacular examples must be that of the

'Paranoid Mass Murderer, Schoolmaster Wagner', described by Robert Gaupp (Hirsch & Shepherd, 1974).

'During the night of 3/4 September, 1913, he first killed his wife and then his four children by making deep cuts in their carotid arteries while they were peacefully asleep. He then travelled by train and bicycle from Stuttgart . . . to Mühlhausen. On the following night he started four different fires in the sleeping village, and then, when the inhabitants were roused by the fires and left their houses to save themselves and rescue their cattle, he fired shots at all the male inhabitants he could see, killing eight outright and severely wounding twelve others as well as two animals. A few brave men struck him down before he could undertake any further destruction; in the excitement he omitted to reload the pistols, each of which contained ten cartridges. He was thus prevented from carrying out the whole of his murderous plan, which was to kill his brother's family in Eglosheim, his birthplace, to burn some other buildings in the village, and then to set fire to the castle in Ludwigsburg, and to shoot himself in the burning castle.

The evening before he killed his family he was his usual friendly polite self, chatting with a teacher's wife . . . commenting on the lovely warm September evenings, and asking his colleague about a certain textbook on physical education. From his writings, we know that 4 years earlier he had already worked out his plan of murder and arson down to the last detail, with a degree of care and deliberation that could not have been more precise' . . .

Ernst Wagner, whose crimes caused an understandable degree of public consternation in Germany, was a well-respected schoolmaster, an educated, intelligent man with a fanatical love of truth—and a network of delusions about the years of imagined persecution and scorn he had suffered while working in Mühlhausen; he spent the rest of his years until his death in 1938 in a mental asylum in Württemberg.

The case of Ernst Wagner, who was without doubt psychotic, was, of course, an extreme one: extreme in the length of planning and the ferocity of the attack, both of which perhaps underline the potential dangerousness of revenge as a motive when arson is the chosen method of retaliation, and particularly in the presence of persecutory delusions. His case was also interesting in that his plan from the beginning clearly entailed suicide. Above all, however, it was the sheer grandiosity of his scheme which is most impressive. Grandiosity, it must be said, is a theme which predominates in the mythology and legend of fire, typified by the *hubris* of Prometheus who stole fire from the gods.

Most cases are in comparison but shadows of the Wagner crime, and the term 'revenge' appears too forceful. 'Grudge' says Barlay (1972) 'is perhaps the best name for the largest mixed bag of motives, ranging from a sudden emotional outburst to a legitimate axe to grind by illegitimate means, from momentary frustration to deep-seated hatred, from rage to jealousy to "getting even"'. Ill-will, malice, or envy may be noted in the activities of frustrated burglars who find nothing up to their expectations in the home of the vicitm, or of some tramps who pay for their hospitality with arson. Perhaps, however, such crimes should be termed sadistic, and their apparent grandiosity —the disproportion between the potential damage and the apparent wrong—is a misperception of these mostly 'pale and insignificant' arsonists, overlooking the accumulated rage induced by the frustration of 'their overall inability to deal with their social, physical, and sexual inferiority' (Lewis & Yarnell, 1951). Below are given the instances of revenge in the literature.

Hurley & Monohan (1962) in a prisoner cohort: 26 per cent; Inciardi (1970) among a cohort of paroled prisoners: 58 per cent; Koson & Dvoskin (1982): 45 per cent, which they divided into 21 per cent revenge against an authority figure, and 24 per cent revenge against a peer; Virkkunen (1974) found hate to be a motive in 50 per cent of schizophrenics and 60 per cent of control arsonists and a previous aggressive trend towards the victim had been shown equally; Virkkunen observed that the schizophrenics were prone to direct things towards themselves and to respond sensitively to even slight offence. Bradford (1982): 38 per cent; Hill *et al.* (1982): 36 per cent; Harmon *et al.* (1985): 37 per cent; and combining revenge and anger: 48 per cent; Yesavage *et al.* (1983) 32 per cent cited vengeance in 'crimes of passion' directed against, for example, the unfaithful wife, the employer who had slighted the employee, or unaffectionate in-laws; one patient in this group set a revenge fire because he was angry at being called retarded; Molnar *et al.* (1984) recorded revenge as the motive in only 16 per cent of those arrested for arson in company with a partner, but in 47 per cent of those arrested on their own; a further 3 per cent of those arrested on their own described their motive as 'anger'. O'Sullivan & Kelleher (1987) found revenge as a motive among 47 per cent and 40 per cent of prisoners and hospital in-patients respectively.

Jealousy

Lewis & Yarnell remark that 'jealousy is usually a central theme in human conflicts'. Their series of 91 men comprised 8 per cent of the total, and were notable perhaps particularly for their dependency; Lewis & Yarnell described their 'personal survival as contingent upon their attachment to a supporting woman' . . . 'Their fires would seem to represent the burning passion of unrequited love, for their favourite object of attack is the clothing or bed of the faithless woman, as plainly expressed by one Negro man who burned his estranged girl's bed, saying "No other man will sleep in the bed I helped pay for" ". Many studies do not, however, separate jealousy from the general category of 'revenge'. Le Couteur (Fry & Le Couteur, 1966), for example, notes that in the 'jealous group' in Broadmoor Hospital, there are many females, but Tennent *et al.* (1971) study of female arsonists in Special Hospitals cites the motive in 18 per cent as 'revenge', when the fire is set in a relative's or boy-friend's home. There are thus few specific references to what might be considered to be a relatively common motive. Hurley & Monohan (1969): 4 per cent; Hill *et al.* (1982): 11 per cent.

INSTRUMENTAL

(Damage, as a reaction, designed as a tactic to achieve an end.)

Criminal

Though barely appearing in the medical literature, politically motivated, and terrorist activity would, for example, be included in this category, as would also arson to cover up crime.

Prins *et al.* (1985) described 1.7 per cent of their series as fire-raising for political purposes. None of the sample, whether prisoners or patients, appeared motivated by 'gain' in O'Sullivan & Kelleher's (1987) study.

The cry for help

Behaviour motivated by a desire for help is of course known by many other, and more commonly pejorative, names such as blackmail or 'manipulative' or 'attention-seeking' behaviour. Fire-setting in this context is extremely coercive, as the weapon is so powerful. Yet it can be viewed alternatively as the activity of a person who feels in other ways powerless to control his environment.

In any behaviour, however, a common feature of motivation may be the presence of more than one reason, existing at different levels. Koson & Dvoskin (1982) for example, describe a case of a schizophrenic who 'set a hotel on fire for a delusional reason but also had a more ulterior and pragmatic motive of getting himself returned to a state hospital'. It would of course be impossible to say which, in the presence of several motives, is the 'truer' or more 'profound'.

Lewis & Yarnell, however, suggest that the inherent nature of fire may in some way determine its use as a vehicle for expressing several different motives, stating: 'Now fire, to belabour the obvious, is a protean elemental force which can be manipulated to express any one or any combination of emotions. A very simple example of a fire doing two things at once, might be the burning of clothing infected from a contagious disease where the fire destroys the clothing, and hopefully, the "germs"; it is destructive to the clothing and "germs", and constructive from the standpoint of community health. An inspection of the motives these fire-setters verbalize often suggests they want the fire to do several different things at once, and this may partially explain why the urge to use fire appears'.

There have been few analyses so far of this aspect of fire-setting, although Prins *et al.* (1985) comment on the difficulty of classifying cases. As an analogy of the complexity of arson it is perhaps simplest to quote Stengel's (1964) analysis of the suicidal act:

'Menninger thought that in committing suicide the individual killed himself, murdered somebody else, and also fulfilled his wish to die. This formula certainly takes account of the aggressive component of the suicidal act, but there are, in addition, motivations which do not spring from the aggressive destructive drives, but from those underlying human relations. There is the desire to bring about a change in other people's feelings towards one, if only posthumously, and also the urge to test fate, in the same way as some children want to find out whether their parents love or hate them. We therefore have to add to Menninger's triad the appeal and the ordeal function of the suicidal act. The two latter spring partly from the urge to self-preservation'.

The 'cry for help' may thus be intrinsically just as much a part of some cases of arson as it is of suicidal activity.

As an example of the complexity of motivation in fire-setting, the interesting case of 'Arson and Moebius' syndrome is quoted (Woolf, 1977). Woolf recorded how this 22-year-old boy, 'with an unusually repellent facial appearance', 'someone who would inevitably arouse feelings of dislike', but of normal intelligence, had managed to survive a normal schooling, an apprenticeship as a cook, and separation from home, until he took up residential catering work in a hospital, with accommodation in the nurses' home. 'Here he encountered teasing and ostracism more cruel and sustained than ever before. His personal life was unhappy, and he failed to make more than transient contacts with the young women living in the home before being crudely and suddenly rejected. He was sent obscene anonymous postcards and became a general laughing stock. None of this unhappiness did he confide to his parents. In the nurses' home he had to share washing facilities with these young women, with whom he failed to make headway, and the room in which their uniforms and underwear were always to be seen drying became a focus for his fantasies and discontent, and preyed upon his mind. On several occasions over a period of about 17 months he burnt and damaged clothing and rubbish in the laundry room and surrounding area. No one was injured, and the total cost of repairs was less than £300'.

Like the case of Ernst Wagner, it is an unusual example. In Court, as a matter of interest, the defendant received a 4-year prison sentence. Should he, principally however, have been classified as 'sexually motivated', 'revenge motivated', or simply, as 'a cry for help?' Was there perhaps also, as Stengel suggests, an 'urge to test fate' in all of these 'little' fires; not in the sense of self-preservation or destruction which Stengel describes, but in the possibly total annihilation of the object? Below are the figures from the adult literature, in which the 'instrumental' or 'cry for help' aspect of arson appears the most prominent.

Inciardi (1970), among paroled prisoners had 6.5 per cent wishing to express dissatisfaction with the institution where they were living. Geller (1984) described fire-setting as a 'communicative' weapon among psychiatric patients, discontented with the location of their current treatment facilities, whether wishing to return to hospital, or to return home in between 17 and 41 per cent of hospital admissions for arson. Among a series of female arsonists, Harmon *et al.* (1985) ascribed the motives of 26 per cent to a cry for help, either in the context of an inappropriate situational response, where delusions or mental illness interfered with the defendant's thought processes, or a depressive illness in which intentional self-destruction was evident. Bradford (1982) defined the motive of 29 per cent of his series as attention-seeking, or a cry for help, and noted that when revenge, cry for help and 'mixed' motives were combined, they covered three-quarters of the whole series. Hurley & Monohan (1969) recorded one case of attempted suicide (2 per cent) and 14 per cent where the motive had been 'destruction of own effects'; Koson & Dvoskin (1982) described the motives of 31 per cent of their series as 'instrumental', in the sense of trying to achieve some external objective in the context of a conflict situation. Molnar *et al.* (1984) regarded 1 per cent of 'partner' arsonists and 6 per cent of 'solo' arsonists as motivated by a death wish, and of the partner and solo groups 5 and 12 per cent respectively expressing a cry for help. Prins *et al.* (1985): 11 per cent. O'Sullivan & Kelleher (1987): 12 per cent of prisoners and 0 per cent of patients motivated by manipulative reasons.

Self-destruction

This topic has been considered under the heading 'Suicide by fire', where the individual figures for motivation are given. It is in many cases extremely difficult to draw a dividing line between the intention behind suicidal and parasuicidal acts, but the category is included for those whose motive is more clearly self-destructive than expressing a cry for help. Self-immolation for political purposes has also been referred to. This motive is only just emerging in the literature: 22 per cent in O'Sullivan & Kelleher's (1987) study.

Children

Fires set by children are usually classified in schemes which classify by motive as 'fires set by children'. Legally this is of course logical, if tautological, since they are not considered old enough to form a criminal intent. Nevertheless, children have motives, and amongst some of the younger children, they might fit more easily under the heading 'a cry for help', and are therefore included in the category 'Instrumental'. Without a clearer understanding, their motives might, of course, be described as the desire to be a 'hero', or to gain power or revenge.

'Hero' type

'These are the fire-setters motivated primarily by vanity—the little men with grandiose social ambitions whose natural equipment dooms them to insignificance. No activity is too bizarre, if it but brings them attention, for they are like adolescents who dream of becoming courageous supermen. They are exhibitionists, pathological liars, but withal glib and ingratiating . . .': Lewis & Yarnell had a series of 6 per cent with this motivation, but they appear to have been common also in the population of Broadmoor Hospital, for Le Couteur (Fry & Le Couteur, 1966) speaks also of 'those who think that their occupation does not show their true value—for example, nurses and night watchmen'.

Lewis & Yarnell included certain female fire-setters as a variety of the 'hero' type, pointing out however, that the role they chose was more often that of the 'heroic victim'. 'Some', for example, 'staged a bizarre fire (usually to their own property, it should be noted) where they appeared, sometimes fantastically dressed for the occasion, as part of the drama'. Although such types are well recognized by physicians, they are not classified as such in the literature, presumably having been included under the category of a 'cry for help'.

Hurley & Monohan (1969): 8 per cent; Prins *et al.* (1985): 2.6 per cent described as 'heroic and vain'; Yesavage *et al.* (1983): included 5 per cent who had been 'incited to the act by others'—presumably with the desire to appear heroic.

CATHARTIC

(Damage inflicted through tension or anger without obvious environmental precipitants.)

Sexual pleasure

Although comprising 3.5 per cent of Lewis & Yarnell's series, this motive for arson appears to be becoming rarer, or is no longer referred to psychiatrists.

Hurley & Monohan (1969): 6 per cent; Virkkunen (1974): 7 per cent of schizophrenics and 3 per cent of controls (a total of three patients) attained clear sexual pleasure and even a state resembling orgasm; Hill *et al.* (1982): 8 per cent; Bradford (1982): 0 per cent; Koson & Dvoskin (1982): 0 per cent; Prins *et al.* (1985): 0 per cent.

Pleasure or excitement, vandalism, boredom, or relief of tension

Bearing in mind the Home Office report on vandalism by fire, this category probably constitutes one of the largest groups of arson, although as can be seen below, references in the literature are not particularly abundant.

Several studies completed since the publication of DSM III in 1980, which contains diagnostic criteria for pyromania, have specifically remarked on the absence of DSM III-defined pyromaniacs among the series of patients described in their studies (e.g., Bradford, 1982; Koson & Dvoskin, 1982). DSM III-pyromania had, however, become extremely limited as a diagnostic category, since it specifically excluded other likely concomitants of arson, such as 'Conduct disorder' or 'Antisocial personality disorder'. As DSM III contains the recommended guidlines for use by American psychiatrists, it would clearly be helpful to know precisely which of the diagnostic criteria have made the diagnosis of 'pyromania' unusable, and whether the new guidelines in DSM IIIR, which do not exclude 'Conduct disorder' or

'Antisocial personality' lead to more frequent use of the diagnosis 'pyromania'. It should be noted in passing that Lewis & Yarnell's (1951) series described 688 men as 'pyromaniacs', but the authors themselves made the proviso that 'many of them offered the excuse of finding themselves controlled by the "irresistible impulse" and, though their stories implied a mixture of all the above motives (revenge, desire to be a hero, etc.), they more often denied such motives, and for this reason we have allowed them to remain loosely classified as pyromaniacs'. DSM IIIR continues specifically to exclude anger or revenge as motives for 'pyromania'.

Nevertheless, the two major elements of the mental state defined by pyromania—the initial build-up of tension, followed by pleasure or release once the fire is under way—would probably justify for present purposes the inclusion under one heading of the various categories 'pleasure, excitement, vandalism, boredom, or relief of tension' which are found in the literature. In the absence of any immediate environmental precipitant, they are considered as an expression of 'initiatory-hostile'—or malicious emotions. Why fire itself should afford their relief remains unknown.

Hurley & Monohan (1969): 12 per cent; Inciardi (1970): among a cohort of paroled prisoners: 22 per cent. Hill *et al.* (1982): 19 per cent described as motivated by pleasure/excitement and 11 per cent had a mischievous affect at the time of fire-setting. Virkkunen (1974) observed that one-third of schizophrenics and controls stayed to watch the fire and thus presumably gained some kind of pleasure from it. Yesavage *et al.* (1983) found that 27 per cent cited pleasure as a motive; Molnar *et al.* (1984) found vandalism and excitement to be the motive of 37 per cent of arsonists arrested with a companion, but only 16 per cent of those arrested on their own. O'Sullivan & Kelleher (1987): 9 per cent described as motivated by 'tension-reduction'.

NO OBVIOUS MOTIVE

For the sake of convenience, three categories of motivation as they occur in the literature have here been grouped under the heading 'no obvious motive', although it has to be said that there is no clear indication of any malicious or hostile intent behind them.

Firstly, several studies, as Koson & Dvoskin (1982) point out, contain the category of 'psychotic' motivation. However, as they remark, delusions are not motives *per se*; they are disorders of thought, whether based on a disorder of perception or affect, beneath whose tangled logic the ordinary motive is occasionally discernible.

Virkkunen (1974) described hallucinations or delusions as the 'principal motive' in 30 per cent of his schizophrenic cases, though stating: 'The motive, more accurately, was a commanding, imperative hallucination in 10 per cent. It was the desire to get into hospital, or prison, in one case; the desire to destroy the voices in another case; to find out the originator of the hallucinations in a third'. In the same vein, a patient in Geller's (1984) study informed the police of the delusion that: 'The devil should do me favours if I set fires', but also told the hospital staff: 'I wanted to upset the group home staff because I didn't think they treated me good'. Thus, in some of the psychotic patients, at one level at least, a vindictive or instrumental motive could have been said to be present. Hill *et al.* (1982): 9 per cent psychotically motivated; Prins *et al.* (1985): 5 per cent; O'Sullivan & Kelleher (1987): 16 per cent.

As a second group, there are those recorded in the literature, whose motives might have been hostile, but who could also have committed arson accidentally, due to a state of confusion: Virkkunen (1974) observed that 17 per cent of this control group had been very drunk, and the fire might then have been accidental, as no rational reason could be revealed. Bradford (1982): 6 per cent; Harmon *et al.* (1985): 11 per cent.

Finally, there is the category 'no obvious motive' itself, as it appears in the literature. It is not of inappreciable size.

Hurley & Monohan (1969): 20 per cent; Virkkunen (1974) found that in 10 per cent of schizophrenics and 7 per cent of controls it was difficult to reveal an accurate motive; Koson & Dvoskin (1982) defined 27 per cent as 'intrinsically motivated'; Hill *et al.* (1982): 42 per cent; Yesavage *et al.* (1983) found that 10 per cent did not know why they had committed the act, and indeed 25 per cent continued to deny that they had done the act; Molnar *et al.* (1984) recorded 'no motive given' among 4 per cent of arsonists arrested with a partner, but 13 per cent of arsonists arrested on their own. Prins *et al.* (1985): 5 per cent had no obvious motive. O'Sullivan & Kelleher (1987): 9 per cent.

In summary then, the motives for arson occurring in the medical literature have been considered under the categories: acquisitive, vindictive, instrumental and malicious. Under those particular headings, motivation has been tabulated as follows:

1. Acquisitive
2. Vindictive
   a. Revenge
   b. Jealousy

3. Instrumental
   a. Criminal
   b. Cry for help
   c. Self-destruction
   d. Children
   e. Hero-type
4. Cathartic
   a. Sexual pleasure
   b. Pleasure, excitement, vandalism, boredom, or relief of tension
5. No obvious motive

Amongst these, the specific categories revenge, cry for help and pleasure/excitement, vandalism, boredom, or relief of tension are numerically the most frequent, although there is a substantial proportion who can only be labelled as 'no obvious motive'.

Summary

'Criminal' motives for arson, such as financial, political, or terrorist activity, are noted to be omitted from the psychiatric literature, though commonly portrayed on the media such as television. Changing social motivations such as the benefits offered to householders following fires, by insurance companies or the welfare state tend also to be overlooked.

In general it may be said that there is confusion over classification of motive in the literature, and a classification is suggested, based on two independent variables of hostile or instrumental and initiatory or reactive aggressive behaviour. Motives from the literature are classified under the headings drawn from these variables, as: Acquisitive, Vindictive, Instrumental, and Cathartic.

Under these four headings, the individual groups found most commonly in the literature are: revenge, cry for help, and pleasure/ excitement, vandalism, boredom, or relief of tension. A substantial proportion are recorded as having no obvious motive. It would appear likely, however, that the quest for any one single motive to explain any one particular behaviour is spurious, and that an approach to classification based on a multi-axial descriptive system would at least begin to clarify the reasons for arson which at present are categorized as 'no obvious motive'.

PERSONALITY OF THE DELIBERATE FIRE-SETTER

Until the development of modern weapons of mass destruction, fire has been the one means by which a single individual could create more havoc and devastation than by using any other tool. Children are taught early of its potentially disastrous consequences (Kafry, 1980). It is no doubt, in part, this willingness to 'play with fire' and to contravene so primitive a social rule, that makes arson so emotive a term and the arsonist so mysterious a figure in popular imagination.

Certainly the potential destruction that may be caused by an arsonist justifies a continuing attitude of extreme caution. However, at the outset it should perhaps be wondered whether a long continued historical interest in pyromania has not in itself contributed to the mystery surrounding the arsonist. Lewis & Yarnell (1951), for example, note that 'for the period preceding 1890, the Index Catalogue for the Surgeon General's Office lists some one hundred and thirty contributors on the subject, a list which does not include the lengthy dissertations to be found in the medical dictionaries and textbooks of the period'. Such an interest may have hallowed the arsonist with mystique, making his offence appear inherently more dreadful than that, for example, of the motorist who travels up a motorway at full speed in thick fog with a coachload of children.

Poetry, too, must have embued the crime with a heritage of romance greater than could be conceivable for any mere twentieth-century offence—for how much more poetic is it to state: 'En chacun de nous dort un incendiare' ('An arsonist lies dormant in all of us') (Marin, quoted by Axberger (1973) in his cross-disciplinary study of arson and fiction) than—'We're all road hogs at heart', or 'There's nothing like a good car crash'. Lewis & Yarnell began their monograph with a chapter entitled: 'Fire: A Universal Symbol': it needs hardly to be said that fire has stood from time immemorial as a symbol for the most powerful concepts known to man. Three well-known quotations may suffice as a reminder of the universality of the image. Fire is often equated with God: 'And the Lord went before them by day in a pillar of a cloud, to lead them the way; and by night in a pillar of fire, to give them light' (Exodus 13:21). It stands for the power of life:

Nature I loved, and next to Nature, Art;
I warmed both hands before the fire of life;
It sinks, and I am ready to depart
(W. S. Landor);

and for the turbulent and unruly passions besetting mankind, 'the heats of our desire',

> Let sense be dumb, let flesh retire,
> Speak through the earthquake, wind, and fire
> O still small voice of calm!
> (J. G. Whittier).

Faced with such a powerful metaphor, it is difficult entirely to discard such overtones in any discussion of arson.

The debate in the medical literature as to why, then, arsonists should choose this particular forbidden weapon has followed several lines. One line of argument, and perhaps the most mundane, is that fire is only one among many tools of destruction, but that it is the one which is attractive since it requires neither physical prowess, nor courage, skill, knowledge, and so forth, and one which, in addition, reaps maximal rewards for the minimal effort. As Griesinger (1867) put it: 'It is a means which is easily employed, and which requires neither great energy of action nor violent determination to make use of'. Fire does not require a licence or a prescription. Fire is thus, in a sense, a natural choice for those who are weak or debilitated in any way. It may also be simply the only available weapon, as for example, to the prisoner locked in his cell with a box of matches.

Some modern constructions of this aspect of fire as a weapon are, however, that the twentieth century, with its ubiquitous central heating and instant gas cookers, no longer entails any personal need for knowledge about fire, which in its most simplistic form is reduced to blowing out candles on a birthday cake or standing behind the barrier at a well organized fireworks display. Such is the lack of knowledge, that even the chip-pan fire is commonly doused with water. In addition, there appears to be a lack of foresight or concern about the hazards of fire in the majority of human beings: fire appliance salesmen are aware, for example, that their easiest sales will occur just after a householder has had a fire, statistically a once-in-a-lifetime event. Fire is therefore not only easy and available, but a present-day arsonist may also choose it through ignorance, lack of experience, and lack of imagination. A comparison of two major programmes for intervention with juvenile fire-setters in the USA, for example, demonstrated that both programmes relied heavily on fire safety education as an intervention measure (Kolko, 1988).

The alternative line of argument is that, far from being a choice randomly determined by simplicity or expedience, the choice of fire-raising is determined by the unconscious significance of the method. Since we have all witnessed some variant of the Guy Fawkes scene, probably on a regular basis, but few are fire-setters, those who indulge in arson must be predetermined by some form of personal experience—such as having been abused as children by being burnt with cigarettes, having friends or relatives die in fires, friends or relatives whose occupation involves fire, by a heavy exposure to hellfire and damnation in the course of religious education, or simply by being brought up in an environment where fire vandalism is a normative experience and a regular group activity (Baizerman & Emshoff, 1984). On this theory, fire-setters are thus conditioned by their previous experiences of fire to choose it as a method. Alternatively again, the symbolic qualities of fire itself may preselect the fire-raiser. Fire has been ascribed the properties of magic and omnipotence; its destructive quality is self-evident. Fire may thus be chosen symbolically though unconsciously, and thus signify the stage of emotional development of the fire-raiser; yet again, these qualities may typify the unconscious needs and wishes of a subject who feels himself trapped in a situation and otherwise impotent to control his environment without the use of a magical, omnipotent, and all-consuming weapon. Great significance may thus be found in the actual choice of fire as a weapon.

None of these explanations is mutually exclusive, for they are merely interpretations of behaviour. As philosophers have noted, an infinite number of theories can be consistent with any set of phenomena. The test of a theoretic formulation lies not in its 'truth', but in its utility. What is wrong with the interpretations, however, is that they are attempting to find one interpretation for what is surely a widespread and heterogeneous offence. An attempt to define the personality of the arsonist is tantamount to asking 'Who is a thief?' The attempt is further bedevilled by the fact that few of those who actually set fires are referred for an assessment, and further by the fact that those studies of personality which have been performed are in one sense predetermined or preselected by the location of the sample, depending on whether they are chosen from psychiatric out-patients or prisons or Special Hospitals, for example.

What then may be said of the personality of different types of fire-setters? Kafry's study (1980) is the only account of the behaviour of 'normal' children and she noted that boys who continued to play with matches—amongst whom any resulting fire appeared to be a matter of chance—were greater 'rascals': they were involved in accidents resulting from hazardous play, and were found to be more mischievous, disobedient, aggressive, and impulsive. These descriptive terms, however, overlooked the positive aspects of their personality: in a different context they would have been regarded as more vivacious, alert, and full of energy; adventurous; endowed with psychological zest, knowledge, and information seeking, as well as showing the negative features of distractibility and poor attention span.

By the time such children are referred to child psychiatrists, the majority of them are acting out other features of deviant behaviour such as lying, stealing, truanting, and fighting, for example, and are labelled 'disorders of conduct' although a small proportion of them demonstrate neurotic symptoms only. Vandersall & Wiener (1970) had observed that among children in their survey, there was no characteristic personality, but subsequent studies have concentrated more specifically on the aggressive nature of the offence. Hypotheses have been offered, for example, that fire-setters may have special problems in expressing aggression, and that fire-setting permits an expression of aggressive feelings without direct confrontation with the victim, or alternatively allows a feeling of control over the environment which the fire-setter has been unable to achieve in other, more interpersonally direct, ways.

Concentrating specifically on the aggressive aspect of the psychopathology of child fire-setters is, for example, the paper of Kolko & Kazdin (1985) who were concerned to establish whether the label 'aggressive' attached itself to fire-setters because the child was particularly aggressive, or whether the attribute derived from the other associated disorders of conduct being displayed by the child, such as lying, stealing, truanting, vandalism, etc. Using several self-report questionnaires for both parents and children to survey the general behaviour of the child, they employed inventories which attempt to define the various facets of 'aggression', such as the Buss–Durkee Inventory (1957) which includes a wide range of behaviours from the directly assaultive to the passive–aggressive mode.

Using this and other inventories of aggressiveness, conduct-disordered fire-setters were rated more aggressive than conduct-disordered non-fire-setters, on some items of the score at levels of statistical significance; with the implication that fire-setting children are 'worse', in the sense of being more 'aggressive', than non-fire-setting children. While the facts established from this survey may very well be true, they do not of course necessarily generalize to the rest of the children outside this psychiatric clinic who are setting fires, as the authors themselves noted. Bearing in mind that 33 per cent of those cautioned or arrested for fire-setting in Britain anyway are under the age of 13, it would be difficult to believe in the existence of such a minefield of undetected aggression in the community amongst children, some of whom are not even arrested by the police. Therefore, considering the results found in the children in this psychiatric study, it might be reasonable to infer that there may be qualities in the parent−child relationship which made the parents more vulnerable and therefore in need of psychiatric assistance with their children. In addition, however, given that fire-setting in the home is probably the single most dangerous act that an average child can perform, it should also be wondered whether the fact of fire-setting does not add a halo-effect to all the other conduct-disordered activities of a child and make him appear more negative than others who are not demonstrating fire-setting behaviour. In short, the results of the study could be more a reflection of family psychopathology than the actual psychopathology of the child and may in addition add to the body of doubt about the validity of self-report questionnaires.

In the literature on adult fire-setters, the same theme of enquiry into patterns of aggression is also evident. Hurley & Monohan's study (1969) of arsonists in Grendon Underwood psychiatric prison began by noting that they are viewed in the Grendon milieu as 'model prisoners', superficially polite, undemanding, and cooperative; they found the arsonists to be more quiet, unassertive, and introverted than controls and conceived of them as passive−aggressive individuals, who avoided direct confrontation, by displaying displaced aggression. Rice & Quinsey (1980), in a survey of arsonists in a facility for dangerous psychiatric patients found a similar lack of social skills, but no difference on psychological tests, however, suggesting over-controlled hostility. Koson & Dvoskin's (1982) study in a maximum security hospital yet again suggested a very aggressive group with a variety of acting-out patterns, primarily involving aggression toward the environment or toward themselves. Lewis & Yarnell had suggested that the arsonist was afraid of the strength of his potential aggressive desires, but was also seriously doubting his ability to attack or fight back; he thus used fire in a passive manner, evading the intent and the possible consequences of his emotions. However, it can only be repeated that no consistent personality emerges from the literature.

But one statement that may be made with certainty is that the 'compulsion' to set fires is not a manifestation of obsessive compulsive neurosis. Gold (1962) points out that the impulse to burn is character-istically episodic; once the impulse to set fire appears, there is very little attempt to resist it; and the impulse is quite compatible with the arsonist's image of himself, causing him little anxiety, and further often producing considerable sensual gratification (Gold, 1962).

In conclusion, it is perhaps as well to return to the symbolism of fire. Topp (1973), Axberger (1973), and others have given helpful accounts of fire as a literary metaphor, all of them noting not only its intensely evocative power as an image, but also that it may stand in great works of literature as a symbol for a wide variety of emotional states—emotions as disparate as divine retribution, reverence, puri-fication, terror, aggressiveness, destructiveness, sexual passion, and perversion. Given then, that there is no common denominator to the symbolism of fire in literature, we are unlikely to find an identikit arsonist in life, more especially since we do not know who the majority of them are.

Summary

Fire is noted historically to have been one of the most potent weapons of mass destruction, and poetically a universal symbol and metaphor for some of the most powerful concepts known to man. Arguments in the literature as to why arsonists should 'play with fire' tend to reflect the outlook of the writer. Such differing perspectives include, on one hand, fire-setting as an easy weapon which requires little skill, and which may be chosen through thoughtlessness or lack of imagination for the consequences. Alternatively, theories on the choice of fire suggest a modelling hypothesis based on experience with fire in childhood. Other explanations for the choice of fire suggest its use for reasons of the unconscious symbolism of fire. None of these explanations is mutually exclusive, since they are inter-pretations of behaviour, coloured by the philosophical outlook of the age in which they were devised.

Modern studies have concentrated on the aggressive aspects of the personality, but without reaching definitive conclusions. Those arson-ists studied in Grendon Underwood psychotherapeutic prison, for example, tend to be non-confronting, passive—aggressive personalties; whilst arsonists from maximum secure environments demonstrate a variety of highly aggressive patterns of behaviour. It is concluded that, in essence, these studies reflect the type of clientele selected as suitable for admission by the particular institution studied, which again demonstrates the fact that arson is not a homogeneous offence, but perpetrated for many different reasons by different types of people.

5 Future research recommendations

Few arsonists are caught. Those who appear to be most easily detected are the ones who were drunk at the time, or mentally retarded. The recommendations for future research are therefore made in the light of the fact that 'known' fire-setters represent only the tip of the iceberg; the 'dark figure' of crime for arson is likely to be very high. The area of relevance to psychiatry would appear to be as follows.

BASIC EPIDEMIOLOGY OF FIRE-SETTING BEHAVIOUR

It is clear that there is very little knowledge of how common or 'normal' a phenomenon fire-setting behaviour is in the general population during childhood and adolescence. A common-sense interpretation of the statistics of the Fire Brigade suggests that it must be a fairly widespread and 'normal' phenomenon. This is speculation, however. It is also clear that we have very little certain knowledge of what should be termed 'fire-setting behaviour' or 'abnormal fire interest', and whether it should include other behaviours such as making false alarm calls and threats to set fires. Even such simple details as, for example, whether there are deliberate fire-setters who do not smoke cigarettes, are missing.

The lack of 'hard' criminological data has implications both for the management and prognosis of patients. One of the main functions of forensic psychiatry lies in gauging prognosis or future dangerousness; such assessments are often criticized as being vague and 'impressionistic'. In terms, too, of understanding the significance of fire-setting behaviour among patients in hospital as well as among those engaging in parasuicidal and self-destructive acts, management would clearly be assisted by a background of definite knowledge and information rather than 'impressions'.

It is likely that any attempt to gain such basic epidemiological data by a 'door-step' survey of the general population would meet with, at best, outright hostility. However, it is not envisaged that there would be any great difficulty in collecting the information from groups who might be motivated to tell the truth, such as intake groups at medical school, theological and teacher training colleges, the police training college at Hendon, and new batches of Army intakes. Given the cover of confidentiality, the Fire Brigade itself would be an interesting source of information.

Within the 'biased sample' of psychiatric populations including, for example, those referred to child and adolescent psychiatrists, general adult psychiatrists, and forensic psychiatrists, it should not be too difficult to conduct a survey of fire-setting behaviour, not only to gain some insight into the basic epidemiology, but also the validity of including other behaviours such as making false alarm calls and making threats to set fires under the rubric of 'abnormal fire interest'. A repetition of Geller & Bertsch's (1985) census study of adult in-patients would be useful.

Studies into the epidemiology of deliberate fire-setting among children and young adolescents should not, in my opinion, be under-taken unless firmly under the aegis of a fire prevention campaign by the Fire Brigade such as is currently occurring in the USA (Kolko, 1988). There seems very little doubt to bodies such as the fire insurance agencies that ignorance about methods of fire prevention and control is fairly widespread in the general population. While it remains controversial whether there is any causal connection between, for example, the portrayal of violence on television programmes and a 'rise in violent behaviour', there appears sufficient evidence—from the documented rise in suicide by fire, and epidemics of fire-setting 'to get back into hospital', to quote only two examples—to support the notion that the young should be regarded as among those vulnerable to suggestion and imitation until proved otherwise, and that academic surveys should be undertaken only in the context of a therapeutic or educational intervention programme.

FIRES SET IN HOSPITAL BY PATIENTS

This is, of course, a matter of practical importance, both in the management of general psychiatric in-patients and the placement of arsonists who are deemed mentally ill.

Hospitals are, by the nature of their occupants, very vulnerable institutions, but through a policy of active prevention, with a District Fire Officer responsible for each district of the Health Service, they have a good record of safety. Nevertheless several notorious hospital fires have occurred. A retrospective survey of fire incidents (fires and false alarms) in one psychiatric hospital concluded that there were sufficient similarities between a fire incident and a violent incident for fire incidents to be included in a hospital register of violent incidents. This finding suggested that fire incidents should be studied prospectively, and that the hospital fire officer should be regarded as an integral part of the multi-disciplinary team for this purpose (Barker *et al.*, 1991). Some of the practical issues of management involve decisions, which at present are made on intuition or personal preference rather than on knowledge or information, on issues such as smoking in hospital, and whether patients who have deliberately set fires should be charged with an offence.

BURNS UNIT STUDY

It is becoming more clear in studies of forensic patients that those who perpetrate acts of violence towards others are also at a greater risk of doing harm to themselves. It is also apparent from this literature review that the incidence of self-injury by fire is greater than we currently appreciate. A study in a burns unit would permit investigation of the psychopathology of those who become victims of burns. The social and demographic features of those who become fatal victims of fire are now becoming fairly well established (Williams, 1984). There are suggestions from the literature, however, that a very considerable incidence of psychopathology may underlie vulnerability to being a burn victim (Noyes *et al.*, 1979). In addition, it would attempt some clearer estimation of the incidence of suicide and parasuicide by fire, replicating the work of Andreasen & Noyes (1975). In addition, however, such a study would investigate the need for a regular liaison psychiatric input to Burns Units, and to evaluate its efficacy. Burns are widely recognized to cause extreme pain and suffering, but there is no established body of knowledge as to their psychotherapy, as is becoming established, for example, in cancer and oncology patients.

ARSONISTS IN PRISON ON REMAND
AND AFTER SENTENCE

Two main topics appear to me to be of importance for future research into deliberate fire-setters. The first involves the issue of future dangerousness; the second, linked issue, is that of the reason for fire as the weapon of choice, which has not so far been addressed in any systematic manner. Both could perhaps be subsumed under the heading 'Motives for arson', which appears the most interesting, the least satisfactorily addressed, and the most difficult, problem in the literature, as observed in a recent study, that of Prins *et al.* (1985).

Because of the seriousness of the offence, arsonists are commonly remanded in custody, and because it is 'good sentencing practice' for arsonists to receive a psychiatric assessment before they are sentenced to determine *inter alia* whether the fire-setting was reckless or intentional, they are routinely interviewed in custody by doctors from the Prison Medical Service. Theoretically, Courts requesting a report on a defendant supply information about the defendant, such as the depositions. In practice, Courts rarely supply such information, and doctors from the Prison Medical Service never complain, principally it appears through an attitude of 'learned helplessness'. A prison survey of arsonists would thus produce not only a large cohort, with a wide range of psychopathology; it should also improve working relationships with the Prison Medical Service who at present are certainly in the front line of care for offender patients.

Although such a study would aim primarily to give a multi-axial classification of arsonists, and thus attempt to delineate various syndromes of arsonists which are of interest to psychiatrists, it would also aim to estimate the extent of psychiatric morbidity among arsonists in prison and the provision of psychiatric care that is made for them, recently criticized in two papers. O'Sullivan & Kelleher (1987), comparing a sample of arsonists from prison and from hospital, commented on the considerable overlap between the two groups, and the apparently 'random and haphazard' manner in which they were allocated to either facility. It is likely that such a study would provide incidental benefits, as for example a better understanding of the relationship of toxic confusional states to full blown cases of Wernicke encephalopathy in alcohol-induced arson.

It is in general my opinion that future studies should concentrate on a descriptive review of arsonists, and that controlled studies should be avoided. The controlled studies that have been undertaken so far have been of great value, in that they have revealed that there is nothing remarkably characteristic about arsonists, as distinct from control groups of offenders. There are at present, however, positive reasons for avoiding studies which attempt to compare arsonists with other types of offenders.

These reasons are inherent in both the nature of arson and the nature of the criminal justice system. The nature of arson is such, for example, that perhaps more than any other crime, it has to be suspected before it is investigated as a crime. Second, it is a crime with a low rate of detection and conviction, and as such a question needing an answer in each case is 'Why did this particular arsonist get caught?' In terms of the seriousness of the particular offence of arson there is a large aspect of chance, since, to use the wisdom of the Fire Brigade, a large fire is one that started small and was not brought under control.

The disparities of the criminal justice system produce widespread vagaries in sampling. Initially, there is a large disparity over the country in the use of the police discretion either to caution or arrest for the same offence (ranging from 45 to 85 per cent in different parts of the country; in itself an interesting area of research would be to examine the characteristics of those who are 'let off' with a caution). At the stage of sentencing, increasing public comment about the necessity for sentencing 'guidelines' for Courts points to the difference in penalties attaching to the same offence. At the stage of selection for various institutions such as Special Hospital for example, the decision-making process of the selection panel at the Department of Health, the final arbiter of selection for Special Hospital until June 1989, could only have been described as highly idiosyncratic. The selection process for Grendon Underwood (psychotherapeutic) Prison lies within the remit of the Prison Medical Service, which is quite distinct from the National Health Service. For reasons such as these it is, in my opinion, at present misguided even to attempt to find a 'control' group when studying arsonists.

A final reason for avoiding control groups lies ultimately in the necessity to concentrate on treatment. Throughout this review there has been hardly any reference to treatment, because there is no known effective treatment, except for obvious cases of illness such as schizophrenia. It is only at the later stage, having acquired the knowledge as to which cases are driven by disease processes, and identified the points of possible therapeutic intervention, that the controlled trial of various types of management strategies in different syndromes of arson, becomes important. Current intervention programmes for juvenile fire-setters, involving a 'multi-disciplinary' approach with an input from the fire prevention services, are a welcome innovation in the USA, but of unproven efficacy.

6 Conclusions

Deliberate fire-setting is one form of aggressive behaviour which occurs in many different guises and contexts, ranging from the pleasures of bonfire night, to terrorist activity. It becomes a criminal offence when the fire-setter is charged with arson under the Criminal Damage Act, 1971, and it is the work of forensic psychiatry to isolate those cases in which the behaviour is driven by disease processes.

Arson is no different from many other categories of criminal activity, in that the term covers the most trivial to the most serious behaviour. However, as an offence it does have characteristics which differentiate it from other types of criminal behaviour. It is, for example, a hallmark of arson that once a fire is started the final *quantum* of damage is largely a matter of chance, which may extend far beyond the original intentions of the fire-setter, and for this reason Courts often request an opinion from the psychiatrist as to whether the fire-setting was reckless or intentional. Arson is not, of course, the only offence with this quality, but it is so prominent a feature, that arson could be said almost to embody the 'urge to test fate'.

It is also somewhat different from other offences, in that it is extremely easy to commit, requiring only enough dexterity to light a match and sufficient mobility to escape being burnt. Perhaps it is not only the damage that may ensue, but also the widespread potential for almost anyone to commit the offence, that makes arson so frightening a behaviour.

Arson, in addition, is distinguished from many other offence categories, in that there needs to be an initial suspicion that the fire-setting was deliberate rather than accidental. There are clearly marked differences in attitude to the origin of fires in different countries, such that, in some jurisdictions, the origin of a fire is regarded as suspicious until proved innocent. In this country a benign view is still taken of the origin of fires; my own opinion is that this attitude must contribute to the low crime rate for arson in Britain, where it is also renowned for the difficulty of obtaining a conviction in the Courts. Another facet of this aspect of the offence of arson is that the inherent difficulties of detection make it an ideal and very dangerous weapon for offending based on 'rational' choice. So few arsonists are detected that arson may be as much the tool of the very intelligent, as it is of the mentally retarded, who are commonly apprehended for it.

In this review I have drawn the conclusion that arson must be a far more common activity than is ever portrayed in the criminal statistics. There is, of course, no direct evidence for this; the conclusion is based on a common-sense interpretation of the fire statistics. However, the conclusion is fully in accord with the 'iceberg phenomenon' of criminal behaviour; it is almost universally held that all detected and prosecuted behaviour represents only the tip of the iceberg of criminal activity. It is also my suspicion that there is a peak age for offending for arson, around the age of 15, which is no different from the peak age of general criminal behaviour. At this age, those setting deliberate fires are termed 'fire vandals' rather than arsonists, and I have suggested that all those deliberately setting fires should be termed arsonists.

A suggestion that all deliberate fire-setters should be termed arsonists is not based on some eccentric desire suddenly to inflate the criminal statistics for arson. Rather, it is based on an attempt to address some of the issues which are of direct relevance to forensic psychiatry. In general terms, the issue of epidemiology is highly significant for prognosis. Such is the difficulty of predicting human behaviour that only one fact can, at present, be taken as a sure guide to gauging future behaviour, and that is the presence of a previous offence. The action of breaking through the barrier between thoughts and words to committing the deed, carries an increased likelihood of repetition. Fire vandals are those who have once broken through the barrier, and their exclusion from the group of deliberate fire-setters termed arsonists clouds this issue of prognosis.

An issue related to prognosis is that of the reason for any particular fire-setter being caught, which, in an offence with a low detection rate, should in my opinion be examined in every case. Conditions carrying a liability to detection, such as alcoholism and mental retardation, appear to me to be over-represented in the criminal statistics. It appears to me, however, not outside the bounds of possibility that detected arsonists may also be over-represented by fire-setters who, at some level at least, recognize a need to be caught and contained. Lewis & Yarnell had recognized a type among their 'pyromaniacs' who settled happily, once in the stable routine of an institution; two recent studies have criticized the apparent failure to deliver care to arsonists who had previously been known to mental health agencies. Within special hospitals there is a well recognized pattern of fire-setting among arsonists 'threatened' with rehabilitation; and the now legal defence that 'she only set fire to get back into hospital' should not therefore appear surprising. Clearly, in an era of community psychiatry, this type of arson, described by Geller as a 'communicative' weapon, will have its own prognostic implications.

A further reason for including all deliberate fire-setters, including fire vandals, under the rubric of arson is to avoid obscuring the issue that behind any behaviour there is an intent, however inchoate, which lies on a continuum from the most banal to the most malevolent. Fire vandals are seen as relatively harmless, as more of a nuisance than a danger, presumably because they 'only' set fire to rubbish, most commonly in derelict inner city areas. This perspective, however, overlooks many social aspects of psychiatry, for it is these very areas which tend to be common breeding grounds not only for delinquent behaviour in general, but also for forensic psychiatric cohorts. Behind the 'mindless' activity of the fire vandal there may be more of a social statement than is superficially apparent. In the section on 'Actual fire-setting behaviour' I have tried to outline the importance, as it has appeared to me, of the details of the fire, such as the materials involved, the time of day and so forth, for an understanding of the intent behind the behaviour. To me, it appears mistaken to exclude the more 'pathetic' attempts at fire-setting from the category arson, for they may be 'pathetic' also, in the sense that they express suffering.

Perhaps, however, the most cogent reason for viewing all deliberate fire-setters as arsonists is to discourage the tendency to view patients as 'Smith the arsonist' or 'Jones the arsonist', a tendency in which one facet of behaviour has become a description of personality. For it is my opinion that the behaviour, arson, should be regarded rather as a symptom or a sign which may indicate the presence of a disease-driven process, or may be amenable to psychiatric intervention. It is evident that various constellations of 'symptoms', or 'syndromes' of arsonists are already known, such as the passive–aggressive individuals commonly found in Grendon Underwood Prison or the self-destructive women in Special Hospitals; suicidal arsonists are increasingly recognized. It would appear more than likely that there are other syndromes of arsonists demonstrating particular constellations of symptoms and behaviours, and their recognition and description would signal progress.

Some of the characteristic features of arsonists that emerge constantly in the medical literature are the facts of a deprived parental background, a low educational status, poor psycho-sexual adjustment, inferior employment record, and alcoholism. The studies that have been produced have been very useful, in that they have excluded any specific factors as the prime driving force or motivation in the aetiology of arson. What they have demonstrated, however, is that these factors are the norm rather than the exception among offender patients, and are in no way particular to arsonists. They establish, in my opinion, the need to advance the study of offending behaviour by abandoning generalities and concentrating on more detailed examination of individuals. Viewed in a historical light, the 'myth' of the triad, enuresis, fire-setting, and cruelty to animals as predictive of future violent behaviour, which is still quoted, may be seen as a paradigm of the quest for, and failure to find, simple certainties in predicting and explaining human behaviour.

The interesting feature of any criminal behaviour is, in my opinion, not the behaviour itself, but the explanation of it; why it happens and what it signifies. It is common in the psychiatric literature dealing with offending behaviour in general to find classifications based on lists of motives; it also appears characteristic that, with the passing of the years, there is a tendency for the lists to lengthen, in what might be described as an anecdotal manner. Any classification of arson based on this system would include motives such as, for example, 'jealous rage' or 'desire to be seen as a hero'. However, my observation is that classifications of other types of aggressive behaviour also contain the same lists of motivation, sometimes with a different wording and sometimes in a different order of priority. Ultimately, although the vocabulary and moral tone have changed, it is difficult to assert that the investigation of human motive has progressed very much further than that of the early Church, which simply proscribed certain emotions as mortal sins, and categorized them as pride, wrath, envy, lust, greed, avarice, and sloth.

The politics of offending behaviour are such that at one level it could be wiser to eschew attempts at a more accurate appraisal of human behaviour. At the most crude level, there remains the threat that doctors will be obliged to revert to pronouncing as 'fit for hanging' those for whom no psychiatric mitigation appears available. All psychiatrists are aware that their patients are stigmatized by society. Forensic psychiatrists are perhaps more aware than others of the potential consequences of being too truthful about, or indeed, giving inaccurate appraisals of, individual human beings; their classifications of behaviour are in this sense pragmatic, serving at least as reminders of motives recognized by Courts and commonly accepted as mitigation for offences.

Nevertheless, it would seem to me important for future work to aim to move towards more theoretical and detailed parameters for classification. In this review I have attempted to classify the motives for arson appearing in the literature on two separate dimensions; one variable attempts to define the source of the aggressive behaviour on the continuum of predominantly reactive to predominantly initiatory behaviour; the second, the type of stimulus to the behaviour, on the continuum between purely hostile and purely instrumental reactions. Such a classification of motive should, in my opinion, be placed within a multi-axial evaluation of the patient, analogous to that used in DSM IIIR, identifying specific areas of psychosocial dysfunction. The outcome of any such multi-axial evaluation is likely to be not simply a better theoretical understanding of behaviour, but also to be more precise in identifying particular areas for intervention; my own impression from this literature review, for example, is that any multi-disciplinary team dealing with offender patients should employ a teacher.

A further axis that, to me, appears necessary in the description of the offender patient is that of the offence itself, which, in the case of arson entails not only a description of the fire but also of knowledge, attitudes, and beliefs in fire. An understanding of the cultural 'mental set' towards a particular offence seems to me important in forming an opinion about its significance. Fire, for example, is universally regarded as dangerous; yet, in practice, in this country, much of society continues apparently ambivalent about its dangers. In 1908, for instance, Parliament found it necessary to insert a clause in the Children and Young Persons Act, making it a criminal offence for a child under 7 to be burnt in the home, such was the extent of injury to young children. It was not until 1952, due in large part to the work of the Colebrooks at the Burns Unit in Birmingham, that Parliament passed a Fireguards Act, making it illegal for fire appliances to be sold without a fireguard. Still today fire prevention salesmen know that their easiest sales will be made after the occurrence of a fire, statistically a once-in-a-lifetime event. The epidemic of suicide by fire recorded in this country in 1978 appears more comprehensible, when viewed in the context of this 'endemic ambivalence' to the dangers of fire.

Arson is a difficult offence to evaluate psychologically, not least because clues as to behaviour and mental state which may be gleaned from the depositions in other offences, have often been destroyed during the course of the fire itself. Nevertheless the symbolic qualities and the 'poetry' of fire provide a handbook in beginning to attempt an understanding of the choice of this particular weapon for aggressive behaviour. There has been as yet no systematic attempt to address the question 'Why fire?'

It is axiomatic in forensic psychiatry that, for whatever reason, patients use deeds in preference to thoughts or words to express an underlying mental state. It is also commonplace that those who have

References

Albrecht, H. (1990). Arson and psychiatry (letter). *N. Z. Med. J.,* **103**, 24.

American Psychiatric Association (1980). *Diagnostic and Statistical Manual of Mental Disorders.* (ed. 3-R). American Psychiatric Association, Washington, DC.

Anderson, R. A., Watson, A. A., & Harland, W. A. (1981). Fire deaths in the Glasgow area. *Med. Sci. Law,* **21**, 175–83.

Andreasen, N. C., & Noyes, R. (1975). Suicide attempted by self-immolation. *Amer. J. Psychiat.,* **132**, 554–6.

Ashton, J. R. & Donnan, S. (1981). Suicide by burning as an epidemic phenomenon: an analysis of 82 deaths and inquests in England and Wales in 1978–9. *Psychol. Med.,* **11**, 735–9.

Awad, G., and Harrison, S. (1976). A female fire-setter: a case report. *J. Nerv. Ment. Dis.,* **63**, 432–7.

Axberger, G. (1973). Arson and fiction: a cross disciplinary study. *Psychiatry,* **36**, 244–65.

Bachelard, G. (1964). *The Psychoanalysis of Fire.* Beacon Press, Boston.

Baizerman, M. & Emshoff, B. (1984). Juvenile fire-setting: the Minneapolis experience. *Fire J.,* **78**, 54–6.

Baker, J. L. (1892). Pyromania. In *Hack Tuke's Dictionary of Psychological Medicine.* Churchill, London.

Barker, A. F., Forshaw, D. M., & Moxom, E. J. (1991). Four year retrospective survey of fire incidents in a psychiatric hospital. *Health Trends,* **23**, 31–2.

Barlay, S. (1972). *Fire: An International Report.* Hamish Hamilton, London.

Barracato, J., & Michelmore, P. (1976). *Arson!* W. W. Norton, New York.

Bender, L. (1953). Fire-setting in children. In *Aggression, Hostility and Anxiety in Children.* C. C. Thomas, Springfield, IL.

Bender, L. (1959). Children and adolescents who have killed. *Amer. J. Psychiat.* **116**, 510–13.

Benians, R. C. (1981). (letter) Conspicuous fire-setting in children. *Brit. J. Psychiat.,* **139**, 366.

Bentley, R. C. (1976). Malicious false alarms, their incidence and causation. *Fire,* August, 142–3.

Block, J. H., Block, J., and Folkman, W. S. (1976). Fire and children: learning survival skills. USA Forest Service Research Paper PSW-119.

Blumberg, N. H. (1981). Arson update: a review of the literature on fire-setting. *Bull. Amer. Acad. Psychiat. Law,* **9**, 255–65.

Boling, I., & Brotman, C. (1975). A fire-setting epidemic in a state mental health centre. *Amer. J. Psychiat.*, **132**, 946–50.

Bourgeois, M. (1969). Suicide par le feu à la manière de bonzes. *Ann. medico-psychol. Rev. psychiat.*, **127**, 116–26.

Bradford, J. M. W. (1982). Arson: a clinical study. *Can. J. Psychiat.*, **27**, 188–93.

Bucknill, J. C., & Hack Tuke, D. (1879). *A Manual of Psychological Medicine.* J & A Churchill, London.

Bumpass, E. R., Fagelman, F. D., & Brix, R. J. (1983). Intervention with children who set fires. *Amer. J. Psychotherapy*, **37**, 328–4.

Buss, A. H., & Durkee, A. (1957). An inventory for assessing different kinds of hostility. *J. Consult. Psychol.*, **21**, 343–9.

Canter, D. (1980). *Fires and Human Behaviour.* John Wiley & Sons, New York.

Carstens, C. (1982). Application of a work penalty threat in the treatment of a case of juvenile fire-setting. *J. Behav. Ther. Exp. Psychiat.*, **13**, 159–61.

Carter, R. E. (1983). The arson epidemic. *Fire Service Today*, March, 18–21.

Clarke, G. (1982). Arson and vandalism. *Fire Prevention*, **144**, 15–19.

Cohen, M. A. A., Aladjem, A. D., Bremin, D., & Ghazi, M. (1990). (letter) Fire-setting by patients with AIDS. *Ann. Intern. Med.*, **112**, 386–7.

Colebrook, L., Colebrook, V., Bull, J. P., & Jackson, D. M. (1951). The prevention of burning accidents. *Lancet*, **2**, 579.

Cooke, R. A., & Ide, R. H. (1985). *Principles of Fire Investigation.* Institution of Fire Engineers, Leicester.

Corbett, J. A. (1979). Psychiatric morbidity and mental retardation. In *Psychiatric Illness and Mental Handicap*, (eds. James, F. E., & Snaith, R. P.) Gaskell, London.

Cowen, P., & Mullen, P. E. (1979). An XYY man. *Brit. J. Psychiat.*, **135**, 78–81.

Craft, M. (1984). Low intelligence, mental handicap and criminality. In *Mentally Abnormal Offenders*, (eds. Craft, M., & Craft, A.) Baillière Tindall, London.

Criminal Damage Act 1971. HMSO, London.

Criminal Statistics (1989). HMSO, London.

Dalton, K. (1961). Menstruation and crime. *Brit. Med. J.*, **ii**, 1752–3.

—— (1980). Cyclical criminal acts in the premenstrual syndrome. *Lancet*, **2**, 1070–1.

Davis, J. (1962). Suicide by fire. *J. Forensic Sci.*, **7**, 393–7.

Denney, E. J. (1979). Trends in malicious fire raising. *Fire Prev.*, **146**, 27–34.

—— (1983). Large fires in schools. *Fire Prev.*, **163**, 16–17.

—— (1984). Trends in malicious fire raising. *Fire Prev.*, **175**, 28–33.

d'Orban , P. T. (1983). Medico-legal aspects of the premenstrual syndrome. *Brit. J. Hosp. Med.*, 404–9.

d'Orban, P. T., & Dalton, K. (1980). Violent crime and the menstrual cycle. *Psychol. Med.,* **10**, 353−9.

Durkheim, E. (1897). *Suicide.* English translation 1952, Routledge & Kegan Paul, London.

Editorial (1980). Hospital fire inquest and report. *Fire,* July, 94.

Editorial (1970). The special dangers of fires in hospitals. *Fire Prev.,* **93**, 14−17.

Edmunds, G. (1978). Judgements of different types of aggressive behaviour. *Brit. J. Social & Clin. Psychol.,* **17**, 121−5.

Ellis, D. P. , & Austin, P. (1971). Menstruation and aggressive behaviour in a correctional centre for women. *J. Crim. Law, Criminology & Police Sci.,* **62**, 388−95.

Esquirol, J. E. D. (1965). *Mental Maladies. A treatise on insanity.* A facsimile of the English edition of 1845. Hafner, London & New York.

Faulk, M. (1978). Arsonists and the psychiatrist. In *Current Themes in Psychiatry,* (eds. Gaind, R., & Hudson, B.). Macmillan, London.

—— (1982). The assessment of dangerousness in arsonists. In *Dangerousness: Psychiatric Assessment and Management,* (eds. Hamilton, J. R., & Freeman, H.) Gaskell, London.

Felthous, A., & Bernard, H. (1979). Enuresis, fire-setting and cruelty to animals: the significance of two thirds of this triad. *J. Forensic Sci.,* **24**, 240−6.

Fenichel, O. (1945). *The Psychoanalytical Theory of Neurosis.* W. W. Norton, New York.

Fine, S., & Louie, D. (1979). Juvenile fire-setters: do the agencies help? *Amer. J. Psychiat.,* **136**, 433−5.

Fineman, K. R. (1980). Fire-setting in childhood and adolescence. *Psychiat. Clin. N. Amer.,* **3**, 483−500.

Fleszar-Szunigajowa, J. (1969). The perpetrators of arson in forensic-psychiatric material. *Po. Med. J.,* **8**, 212−19.

Foust, L. (1979). The legal significance of clinical formulations of fire-setting behaviour. *Int. J. Law Psychiat.,* **2**, 371−87.

Freud, S. (1932). The acquisition of power over fire. *Int. J. Psychoanalysis,* **13**, 405−10.

—— (1977). *Case Histories I.* Pelican Books, London.

Fry, F., & Le Couteur, E. (1966). Arson. *Medico-legal J.,* **34**, 108−21.

Future Fire Policy: A Consultative Document (1980). HMSO, London.

Gaupp, R. (1974). The scientific significance of the case of Ernst Wagner. In *Themes and Variations in European Psychiatry,* (eds. Hirsch, S. R., & Shepherd, M.). University Press, VA.

Geller, J. (1984). Arson: an unforeseen sequela of deinstitutionalization. *Amer. J. Psychiat.,* **141**, 504−8.

—— , & Bertsch, G. (1985). Fire-setting behaviour in the histories of a state hospital population. *Amer. J. Psychiat.,* **142**, 464−8.

Gerard, M. (1939). Enuresis. *Amer. J. Orthopsychiat.,* **IX**, 1.

Gibbens, T. C., & Robertson, G. (1983). A survey of the criminal careers of hospital order patients. *Brit. J. Psychiat.,* **143**, 362−9.

—— (1983). A survey of the criminal careers of restriction order patients. *Brit. J. Psychiat.*, **143**, 370–5.

Gold, J. (1962). Psychiatric profile of the fire-setter. *J. Forensic Sci.*, **7**, 404–17.

Griesinger, W. (1867). *Mental Pathology and Therapeutics*, (trans. from 2nd edn) The New Sydenham Society, London.

Grinstein, A. (1952). Stages in the development of control over fire. *Int. J. Psychoanal.*, **33**, 416–20.

Gruber, A. R., Heck, E. T., & Mintzer, E. (1981). Children who set fires; some background and behavioural characteristics. *Amer. J. Orthopsychiatr.*, **51**, 484–8.

Gunderson, J. (1974). Management of manic states: the problems of fire-setting. *Psychiatry*, **37**, 137–46.

Harmon, R. B., Rosner, R., & Wiederlight, M. (1985). Women and arson: a demographic study. *J. Forensic Sci.*, **30**, 467–77.

Heath, G. A., Gayton, W. F., & Hardesty, V. A. (1976). Childhood fire-setting. *Can. Psychiat. Assoc. J.*, **21**, 229–37.

——, Hardesty, V. A., & Goldfine, P. E. (1983). Childhood fire-setting: an empirical study. *J. Amer. Acad. Child Psychiat.*, **22**, 370–4.

Heller, M. S., Ehrlich, S. M., & Lester, D. (1984). Childhood cruelty to animals, fire-setting and enuresis as correlates of competence to stand trial. *J. Gen. Psychol.*, **110**, 151–3.

Hellman, D., & Blackman, N. (1966). Enuresis, fire-setting and cruelty to animals: a triad predictive of adult crime. *Amer. J. Psychiat.*, **122**, 1431–5.

Herjanic, M., Henn, F. A., & Vanderpeal, R. H. (1977). Forensic psychiatry: female offenders. *Amer. J. Psychiat.*, **134**, 556–8.

Hill, R. W., Langevin, R., Paitich, D., Handy, L., Russon, A., & Wilkinson, L. (1982). Is arson an aggressive act or a property offence? A controlled study of psychiatric referrals. *Can. J. Psychiat.*, **27**, 648–54.

Holland, C. J. (1969). Elimination by the parents of fire-setting behaviour in a 7 year old boy. *Behav. Research Ther.*, **7**, 137.

Home Office Working Party (1980). Seminar on fires caused by vandalism.

Hunter, H. (1979). Forensic psychiatry and mental handicap: a clinical approach. In *Psychiatric Illness and Mental Handicap*, (eds. James, F. E., & Snaith, R. P.) Gaskell Press, London.

Hurley, W., & Monohan, T. M. (1969). Arson: the criminal and the crime. *Brit. J. Criminol.*, **9**, 4–21.

Inciardi, J. A. (1970). The adult fire-setter: a typology. *Criminology*, **8**, 145–55.

Jacobson, R. R. (1985a). Child fire-setters: a clinical investigation. *J. Child Psychol. Psychiat.*, **26**, 759–68.

—— (1985b). The subclassification of child fire-setters. *J. Child Psychol. Psychiat.*, **26**, 769–75.

——, Jackson, M., & Berelowitz, M. (1986). Self-incineration: a controlled comparison of in-patient suicide attempts. *Psychol. Med.*, **16**, 107–16.

Jones, F. D. (1981). Therapy for fire-setters (letter). *Amer. J. Psychiat.*, **138**, 261−2.

Justice, B., Justice, R., & Kraft, I. (1974). Early warning signs of violence: is a triad enough? *Amer. J. Psychiat.*, **131**, 457−9.

Kafry, D. (1980). Playing with matches: children and fire. In *Fires and Human Behaviour*, (ed. Canter, D.). John Wiley & Sons, New York.

Kaler, S. G., White, B. J., & Kruesi, M. J. P. (1989). (letter) Fire-setting and Klinefelter syndrome. *Pediatrics*, **84**, 749−50.

Kammerer, T. H., Singer, L., & Michel, D. (1967). Les incendiaires. Étude criminologique et psychologique de 72 cas. *Ann. med.-psychol.*, **125**, 687−716.

Kanner, L. (1957). *Child Psychiatry.* C. C. Thomas, Springfield, IL.

Kaufman, I., Heins, L., & Reiser, D. (1961). The re-evaluation of the psycho-dynamics of fire-setting. *Amer. J. Orthopsychiat.*, **31**, 123−36.

Klein, M. (1932). *The Psycho-Analysis of Children.* Hogarth Press, London.

Koles, M. R., & Jenson, W. R. (1985). Comprehensive treatment of chronic fire setting in a severely disordered boy. *J. Behav. Ther. Exp. Psychiat.*, **16**, 81−5.

Kolko, D. J. (1983). Multicomponent parental treatment of fire-setting in a six year old boy. *J. Behav. Ther. Exp. Psychiat.*, **14**, 349−53.

—— (1988). Community interventions for juvenile fire-setters: a survey of two national programs. *Hosp. Commun. Psychiat.*, **39**, 73−9.

——, & Kazdin, A. E. (1985). Aggression and psychopathology in childhood fire-setters: parent & child reports. *J. Consult. Clin. Psychol.*, **53**, 377−85.

——, ——, (1988). Prevalence of fire-setting and related behaviours among child psychiatric patients. *J. Consult. Clin. Psychol.*, **56**, 628−30.

——, ——, (1989). Assessment of dimensions of childhood fire-setting among patients and non-patients: The fire-setting risk interview. *J. Abn. Child Psychol.*, **17**, 157−76.

Kosky, R. J. (1983). Childhood suicidal behaviour. *J. Child Psychol. Psychiat.*, **24**, 457−68.

——, & Silburn, S. (1984). Children who light fires: a comparison between fire-setters and non-fire-setters referred to a child psychiatric outpatient service. *Aus. N.Z. J. Psychiat.*, **18**, 251−5.

Koson, D. F., & Dvoskin, J. (1982). Arson: a diagnostic study. *Bull. Amer. Acad. Psychiat. Law*, **10**, 19−49.

Kuhnley, E. J., Hendren, D. O., & Quinland, D. M. (1982). Fire-setting by children. *J. Amer. Acad. Child Psychiat.*, **21**, 560−3.

Lande, S. D. (1980). A combination of orgasmic reconditioning and covert sensitization in the treatment of a fire-fetish. *J. Behav. Ther. Exp. Psychiat.*, **11**, 291−6.

Lawrence, J. C., & Melinek, S. J. (1979). Hospital records analysed to find medical costs of fire injuries. *Fire*, **72**, 94−6.

Levin, B. (1976). Psychological characteristics of fire-setters. *Fire J.*, **70**, 36−40.

Lewis, N. (1966). Pathological fire-setting and sexual motivation. In *Sexual Behaviour and the Law*. (ed. Slovenko, R.) C. C. Thomas, Springfield, IL.

Lewis, N. D. C., & Yarnell, H. (1951). *Pathological Fire-Setting. Nervous & Mental Disease Monographs No 82*, New York.

Lowenstein, L. F. (1981). The diagnosis of child arsonists. *Acta Paedopsychiat.*, **47**, 151–4.

—— (1989). The aetiology, diagnosis and treatment of the fire-setting behaviour of children. *Child Psychiat. Human Devel.*, **19**, 186–95.

MacDonald, J. (1963). The threat to kill. *Amer. J. Psychiat.*, **120**, 125–30.

—— (1977). *Bombers and Fire-setters*. C. C. Thomas, Springfield, IL.

Macht, L. B., & Mack, J. E. (1968). The fire-setter syndrome. *Psychiatry*, **31**, 277–88.

Mahon, B. H. (1978). *Fires in Hospitals*. Unpublished results, Fire Research Station, Borehamwood.

Marc, M. (1833). Considerations medico-legales sur la monomanie et particulièrement sur la monomanie incendiaire. *Annales d'hygiene publique et de medicine legale*, **10**, 367–484.

Maudsley, H. (1896). *Responsibility in Mental Disease*. Appleton, New York.

Mayhew, P., & Clarke, R. (1982). Vandalism and its prevention. In *Developments in the Study of Criminal Behaviour*, (ed. Feldman, P.) John Wiley & Sons, London.

McClure, G. M. G. (1984). Trends in the suicide rate for England & Wales 1975–80. *Brit. J. Psychiat.*, **144**, 119–26.

McGuire, R. J., Carlisle, J. M., & Young, B. G. (1965). Sexual deviations as conditioned behaviour: a hypothesis. *Behav. Res. Ther.*, **2**, 185–90.

McKerracher, D. W., & Dacre, A. J. I. (1966). A study of arsonists in a special security hospital. *Brit. J. Psychiat.*, **112**, 1151–4.

McKinney, C. D. (1983). Stopping the continuing circle of juvenile fire raising. *Fire Prev.*, **163**, 23–5.

Michaels, J. J., & Steinberg, A. (1952). Persistent enuresis and juvenile delinquency. *Brit. J. Delinq.*, **3**, 114–23.

Modan, B., Nissenkorn, I., & Lewkowski, S. R. (1970). Comparative epidemiological aspects of suicide and attempted suicide in Israel. *Amer. J. Epidemiol.*, **91**, 383–9.

Molnar, G., Keitner, L., & Harwood, B. T. (1984). A comparison of partner and solo arsonists. *J. Forensic Sci.*, **29**, 574–83.

Mönkemöller, X. (1912). Zur Psychopathologie des Brandstifters. *Hans Gross Archiv für Kriminal-Anthropologie und Kriminalistik*, **XLVIII**, 193–312.

Newton, J. (1976). Suicide by fire. *Med. Sci. Law*, **16**, 177–9.

Noyes, R., Frye, S. J., Slymen, J., & Canter, A. (1979). Stressful life events and burn injuries. *J. Trauma*, **19**, 141–4.

Nurcombe, B. (1964). Children who set fires. *Med. J. Aus.*, **1**, 579–84.

Nuttall, C. P., Barnard, E. E., Fowles, A. J., & Frost, A. (1977). *Parole in England & Wales*. Home Office Research Study No. 38. HMSO.

O'Gorman, G. (1979). Abnormalities of movement. In *Psychiatric Illness and Mental Handicap,* (eds. James, F. E., & Snaith, R. P.). Gaskell Press, London.

O'Sullivan, G. H., & Kelleher, M. J. (1987). A study of fire-setters in the South-West of Ireland. *Brit. J. Psychiat.,* **151**, 818–23.

Pao, P. N. (1969). The syndrome of delicate self-cutting. *Brit. J. Med. Psychol.,* **42**, 195–206.

Parker, E. (1974). *Survey of incapacity associated with mental handicap at Rampton and Moss Side Special Hospitals.* SHRU Report, No. 11.

Perr, I. (1979). Comments on arson. *J. Forensic Sci.,* **24**, 885–9.

Police and Criminal Evidence Act (1984). s.66: Code of Practice. HMSO, London.

Power, D. J. (1969). Subnormality and crime I and II. *Med. Sci. Law,* **9**, 83–93, 162–71.

Pratt, P. (1974). Arson, the neglected crime. Observer Magazine 3.3.74.

Price, C. & Caplan, J. (1977). *The Confait Confessions.* Boyars, London.

Prins, H. (1976). Remands for psychiatric reports. *Med. Sci. Law,* **16**, 129–38.

—— (1978). 'Their candles are all out (Macbeth): or are they': Some reflections on arson and arsonists. *R. Soc. Health J.,* **98**, 191–5.

—— (1980). Fire-raising and fire-raisers. In *Offenders, Deviants, or Patients?* Tavistock, London.

——, Tennent, G., & Trick, K. (1985). Motives for arson (fire-raising). *Med. Sci. Law,* **25**, 275–8.

Quinsey, V. L., Arnold, L. S., & Pruesse, M. G. (1980). MMPI profiles of men referred for a pretrial psychiatric assessment as a function of offence type. *J. Clin. Psychol.,* **36**, 410–16.

——, Chaplin, T. C., and Upfold, D. (1989). Arson and sexual arousal to fire-setting: correlation unsupported. *J. Behav. Ther. Exp. Psychiat.,* **20**, 203–9.

Report of Her Majesty's Chief Inspector of Fire Services (1989). HMSO, London.

Rice, M. E., & Chaplin, T. (1979). Social skills training for hospitalized male arsonists. *J. Behav. Ther. Exp. Psychiat.,* **10**, 105–8.

——, & Quinsey, V. L. (1980). Assessment and training of social competence in dangerous psychiatric patients. *Int. J. Law Psychiat.,* **3**, 371–90.

Rider, A. D. (1980). The fire-setter: a psychological profile. *F.B.I. Law Enforcement Bulletin.* June, July, August.

Robbins, E., Herman, M., and Robbins, L. (1969). Sex and arson. Is there a relation? *Med. aspects human sex.,* **3**, 57–64.

Robertson, G. (1981). The extent and pattern of crime amonst mentally handicapped offenders. *Apex. J. Brit. Inst. Ment. Hand.,* **9**, 100–3.

Rosenstock, H. A., Holland, A., & Jones, P. H. (1980). Fire-setting on an adolescent inpatient unit: an analysis. *J. Clin. Psychol.,* **41**, 20–2.

Royer, F. L., Flynn, W. F., & Osadca, B. S. (1971). Case history: aversion therapy for fire-setting by a deteriorated schizophrenic. *Behav. Ther.,* **2**, 229–32.

Sakheim, G., Vigeor, M., Gordon, M., & Helprin, L. (1985). A psychological profile of juvenile fire-setters in residential treatment. *Child Welfare*, **65**, 495–503.

Sapsford, R. J., Banks, C., & Smith, D. D. (1978). Arsonists in prison. *Med. Sci. Law*, **18**, 247–54.

Savage, G. H. (1881). Moral insanity. *J. Ment. Sci.*, July.

Scott, D. (1974). *Fire and Fire-raisers*. Duckworth, London.

—— (1977). Malicious fire-raising. *Practitioner*, **218**, 812–17.

—— (1978). The problem of malicious fire-raising. *Brit. J. Hosp. Med.*, **19**, 259–63.

Silverman, J. S. (1957). Phenomenology and thinking disorder in some fire-setting children. *Psychiat. Quart. Suppl.*, **31**, 11–25.

Simmel, E. (1949). Incendiarism. In *Searchlights on Delinquency*, (ed. Eissler, K. E.) International University Press, New York.

Soothill, K. L., & Pope, P. J. (1973). Arson: a twenty year cohort study. *Med. Sci. Law*, **13**, 127–38.

Stawar, T. L. (1976). Fable mod: operantly structured fantasies as an adjunct in the modification of fire-setting behaviour. *J. Behav. Ther. Exp. Psychiat.*, **7**, 285–7.

Stekel, W. (1924). *Peculiarities of Behaviour, vol. 2*. (trans. van Teslar) Williams & Norgate, London.

Stengel, E. (1964). *Suicide and Attempted Suicide*. Penguin, London.

Stewart, M. A., & Culver, K. W. (1982). Children who set fires: the clinical picture and follow-up. *Brit. J. Psychiat.*, **140**, 357–63.

Stollard, P. (1983). The coding and analysis of fire reports. Unpublished thesis, University of Edinburgh.

Strachan, J. G. (1981). Conspicious fire-setting in children. *Brit. J. Psychiat.*, **138**, 26–9.

Tardiff, K. (1982). A survey of five types of dangerous behaviour among chronic psychiatric patients. *Bull. Amer. Acad. Psychiat. Law*, **10**, 177–82.

Taylor, P. J., & Gunn, J. (1984). Violence and psychosis. I: Risk of violence among psychotic men. *Brit. Med. J.*, **288**, 1945–9.

—— (1984). Violence and psychosis II: Effect of psychiatric diagnosis on conviction and sentencing of prisoners. *Brit. Med. J.*, **289**, 9–12.

Teague, P. E. (1976). Arson: the growing problem. *Fire J.*, March.

Tennent, T. G., McQuaid, A., Loughnane, T., & Hands, A. J. (1971). Female arsonists. *Brit. J. Psychiat.*, **119**, 497–502.

Thomas, D. (1988). *Current Sentencing Practice*. Sweet & Maxwell, London.

Topp, D. (1973). Fire as a symbol and as a weapon of death. *Med. Sci. Law*, **13**, 79–86.

—— (1979). Suicide in prison. *Brit. J. Psychiat.*, **134**, 24–7.

Tucker, R., & Cornwall, T. (1977). Mother-son folie à deux: a case of attempted patricide. *Amer. J. Psychiat.*, **134**, 1146–7.

United States Fire Administration (1979). *Report to the Congress: Arson: the Federal Role in Arson Prevention and Management*. Federal Emergency Management Agency, Washington.

Vandersall, T. A., & Wiener, J. M. (1970). Children who set fires. *Arch. Gen. Psychiat.*, **20**, 63–71.

Virkkunen, M. (1974). On arson committed by schizophrenics. *Acta Psychiat. Scand.*, **50**, 152–60.

—— (1984). Reactive hypoglycaemic tendency among arsonists. *Acta Psychiat. Scand.*, **69**, 445–52.

——, de Jong, J., Bartko, J., & Linnoila, M. (1989a). Psychobiological concomitants of history of suicide attempts among violent offenders and impulsive fire-setters. *Arch. Gen. Psychiat.*, **46**, 604–6.

——, ——, ——, Goodwin, F. K., & Linnoila, M. (1989b). Relationship of psychobiological variables to recidivism in violent offenders and impulsive fire-setters. A follow up study. *Arch. Gen. Psychiat.*, **46**, 600–3.

Vreeland, R. G., & Levin, B. M. (1980). Psychological aspects of fire-setting. In *Fires and Human Behaviour*, (ed. Canter, D.). Center for Fire Research, National Bureau of Standards, Washington, DC.

——, & Waller, M. B. (1978). *The Psychology of Fire-Setting: a Review and Appraisal*. US Dept of Commerce, National Bureau of Standards.

——, ——, (1979). Personality theory and fire-setting: an elaboration of a psychological model. US Dept of Commerce, National Bureau of Standards.

Walker, N., & McCabe, S. (1973). *Crime and Insanity in England*. University Press, Edinburgh.

Wax, D., & Haddox, V. (1974). Enuresis, fire-setting & animal cruelty in male adolescence. *J. Psychiat. Law*, **2**, 45–71.

Webb, N. B., Sakheim, G. A., Towns-Miranda, L., & Wagner, C. R. (1990). Collaborative treatment of juvenile fire-setters: assessment and outreach. *Amer. J. Orthopsychiat.*, **60**, 305–10.

West, D. J., & Walk, A. (1977). *Daniel McNaughton: his Trial and the Aftermath*. Gaskell, London.

Williams, A. W. (1984). *Domestic Fire Deaths*. Building Research Establishment information paper, Borehamwood, IP 23/84.

Williams, G. L. (1953). *Criminal Law*. Stevens & Sons, London.

Winget,C., & Whitman, R. (1973). Coping with problems: attitudes towards children who set fires. *Amer. J. Psychiat.*, **130**, 442–5.

Woolf, P. (1977). Arson & Moebius syndrome: a case study of stigmatization. *Med. Sci. Law*, **17**, 68–70.

Yarnell, H. (1940). Fire-setting in children. *Amer. J. Orthopsychiat.*, **10**, 272–86.

Yesavage, J. A., Benezech, M. , Ceccaldi, P., Bourgeois, M., & Addad,M. (1983). Arson in mentally ill and criminal populations. *J. Clin. Psychiat.*, **44**, 128–30.

Zemishlany, Z., Weinberger, A., Ben-Bassat, M., & Mell, H. (1987). An epidemic of suicide attempts by burning in a psychiatric hospital. *Brit. J. Psychiat.*, **150**, 704–6.

Index